*The Path to Love is
the Practice of Love*

The Path to Love is the Practice of Love

An Introduction to Spirituality with Self-Help Exercises For Small Groups

Carol Riddell

FINDHORN Press

ISBN 1 899171 20 7

British Library Cataloguing-in-Publication Data.
A catalogue record for this book is available
from the British Library.

Set in Palatino by Findhorn Press
Cover illustration © Harley Miller 1995
Author photograph by Findhorn Foundation Visual Arts
Cover design by Posthouse Printing
Printed and bound by WSOY, Finland

Published by
Findhorn Press
The Park, Findhorn,
Forres IV36 0TZ, Scotland
01309-690582 / fax 690036
e-mail thierry@findhorn.org

Acknowledgements

Above all, to 'Swami', Bhagavan Sri Sathya Sai Baba, Source, Inspiration, Guide, Supporter, Friend, Divinity. If I look to Him, He looks to me. And even if I forget, He looks to me.

The basis of this book was written during a three months' stay gifted to me by Albert and Anneliese Harloff at their beautiful centre, 'A Rochinha' at Ponta do Sol on Madeira, an inspiring location. We are always together in our hearts.

Henk, Marianne, Arendt and Hanka Van der Sluis gave the house 'Taigh Sith' on the Ross of Mull, for me to live in during typing up, as part of the 'Highland Renewal' Project we are all engaged in. Charles and Heather Murphy were there to support me as I began the text preparation and Charles did some initial revision. When they went south for a time, Iris Urfer gave me her love and support. The detailed criticism of Sandra Kramer and Lynn Barton stimulated me to present the book in this form.

The Findhorn Foundation and its Erraid Community have given me so much over the years! So many friends, so much unstinting support!

Charlette, the indefatigable 'Kaypro Computer' has written her third book, and Brother HRII, my printer, his first (as far as I know.) Thank you, everyone.

Dedicated in Love, Humility and Gratitude to

BHAGAVAN SRI SATHYA SAI BABA.

Other Books by Carol Riddell:

• Approaching Sociology (with M.Coulson)
• The Findhorn Community
• Gifts of Divine Love (with Marianne Kersten.) (In preparation.)

Foreword

Many people are now seeking to reach a state of divine and unconditional love. Carol Riddell's book offers constructive, common sense help in reaching this ideal and how to incorporate it into everyday living. She leads us to discover the love within each one of us, and stretches our consciousness to reach that only real source of happiness — Love.

The exercises are excellent, and will be invaluable not only for groups but also for the individual on the path to unconditional love. I believe the meditations, some of which I personally use and find extremely powerful, will also facilitate the reader in their inner search for their divine centre. The desire to reach this centre leads us on the path to love, and the way to reach this path is the practice of love, through service, devotion and stillness. Let service come from wholeness, not lack. Let devotion be the practice of love, and the practice of love be stillness.

Let all you do and all the words you express come from love. The time for love is now, for now is all the time we have.

Eileen Caddy

Contents

Introduction

This book explains the meaning of a spiritual life, and provides a way for people to get together with like-minded friends to practice its principles. Through understanding and practice, one can transform daily life, give meaning to one's experiences, and find happiness in the service of others.

There is little 'theology' or narrowing dogmatism. The teachings can equally apply to Christians, Buddhists, Moslems, Jews, Hindus or Humanists, as long as one accepts that the essential principle of the cosmos is love, a love which is both detached and personal, all-pervasive yet specific. The various religions are the structures and social supports through which the search for truth can be channelled. All are, ultimately, equally valid; yet, in as far as they are social constructs, flawed.

The guidance in this book is 'channelled', a technique for accessing a higher wisdom that can be learned (see exercise 11). The exercises have been tested over a period of four years in workshops in several European countries and at the Findhorn Foundation. Several self-help groups have already used them.

The dominant 'religion' of this age is materialism, a world-wide doctrine with many 'priests'. Its consequences are disillusionment, cynicism and, in the worst cases, self-destruction. Finding a way past materialism is the challenge of this era. As a result of my own experiences, I have become confident that humanity will find the way. This manual is a contribution to that end. It is the result of 20 years of training and experience in Zen meditation, therapy, psychic studies, at the Findhorn

Foundation and as a devotee of Sathya Sai Baba, the great Indian spiritual teacher.

As always with such texts, work with it carefully, but critically. It will help you along your own path to true happiness in life.

Guidance

The Path to Love

---

the Practice of Love

Contents

Who doesn't want happiness in life? People every-where, whatever the task they are engaged in, hope for it. They define their aim in many different ways. For one, it is having a new car or computer; for another, own-ing a piece of land. It may demand possession of a loved one, or an increase in power and prestige. Every human desire you can think of is projected as a potential source of happiness.

Many dream of happiness in social terms: they believe 'society' or 'people' could be happy through belonging to this or that institution - such as the church, or 'democratic society' — or through social transformation.

None of these individuals and social groups have found what they seek. They go through life searching. Some are convinced they have discovered the source of happiness; only a little more will give fulfilment - another (newer) car, computer, wife, husband, project. Others cajole — only a little more struggle, violence, obedience . . . and happiness will be there for the populace.

As people get older, many become disillusioned. They feel happiness is a death-right, only existing when unpleasant earthly duties have been fulfilled. Others resign themselves to obligation and dullness, resentful of those who so foolishly seek an unattainable goal. They are mistaken. Happiness *is* the birthright of every human, but it is a state of being, not a state of achievement or pos-session. It has to be realised. You have it now, but are unaware of it because of the way you perceive and define the world around you. It is inherent, all-pervasive. It is, *now*, and remains so, irrespective of circumstance. Hap-piness is not in another bucket, so to speak. It is in the bucket in your hand, hidden under the sand of attitude

and world view. It is perception that needs to be transformed. The first great spiritual challenge is to shift the
focus of longings from a future state of acquiring to a present state of *recovering, uncovering*.

To take this important spiritual step requires an act
of faith. Old thought patterns whisper: 'If I don't feel
happy right now, how can I actually be happy - that denies
my own experience.' On the contrary! It has to be
affirmed: 'Though I don't feel happy right now, it is due
to the way I see things.' It is not such an easy step to take
and maintain; it is not easy at first to trust. There is help
there; but even accepting that can be scary. Yet it is this
change in attitude which leads beyond knowledge to wisdom itself.

The Basis of Happiness is Love.

It can be affirmed: Love alone exists; all else is secondary. Love expands and presents itself as *forms*. Physicality, thought and expression, are all, in their essence, love. The entire universe is composed of and constructed of love. Love is the natural organising principle of human existence. The expression of love is necessary in relationship and the growth of human awareness. Here, then, are three great spiritual truths:

• The physical universe is love clothed in *form*.
• The way of the universe is love organised in *structure*.
• Conscious life results from love expressed in *relationship*.

The third truth provides the link between human consciousness and the true source of happiness. It is like the key which opens the door to happiness. We will return to it later.

Love is a quality — but one unlike any other. Since love is the basis of everything, it has no opposite. If it were to have one, it would not be something like 'hate', which is merely love distorted, but 'nothingness', which is an irrelevance.

In the spiritual sense, all consciousness that does not experience existence as love is illusory. As soon as love takes the form of human beings, those same humans learn to experience life in ways that hide the love from which they were created. The social construction of human existence itself builds this 'illusion' in. Although all the objects you may experience with your senses are actually love, without their differentiation into forms and names, consciousness itself would be impossible. Although human life requires the illusion of form, it is possible to regain the experience that love is the basis of every form.

Love, as a quality, is not neutral. In human experience it translates itself as feeling. This 'feeling quality' of love in human relationships — whether to parent, spouse, child, pet, nature or God — is genuine 'happiness'. The more one experiences love, the more happiness there is. Eventually, happiness becomes 'bliss'.

Beyond bliss is 'ecstasy', which describes the experience of the whole of creation as love. To penetrate the illusion that there is 'not-love' is ultimate fulfilment — to reach enlightenment. It requires that everything that exists be experienced as love. Once one is completely illusion-free, harm and hurt to others would just be unthinkable. But as human beings develop, the practice of love and its expansion to wider and wider areas of life lead to steadily increasing happiness.

Here is a simple example:

If you work in an office with five people and like two of them, are indifferent to two and dislike one, we can give you a 'happiness quotient' of +2 -1 = 1.

If you change your attitude so you can like three, remain indifferent to one and still hate one, your 'hq' will then be +3 -1 = 2. By changing a little more so you are indifferent to the one you disliked, your 'hq' then becomes 3.

It rises to 5 when you can like them all.

Let's suppose your 'transformation' *doubles* the intensity of your 'liking' by increasing its love content. Your happiness quotient will then shoot up to 10.

Finally, to find enlightenment, you transform yourself so that you experience love for all humanity and the created universe, without exception. Your 'happiness quotient' is then infinite!

How do you transform yourself? The first thing you have to do is to determine to try and lovingness increases. Then, try to accept that all is ultimately love, even if this seems abstract at first. You are now on your way to the deepest truth of all great religious belief - God is love, and love is God.

Since the truth is that the basis of all existence is love, you also are love. If you do not experience yourself as love, your experience of the rest of creation as love will not be perfect. The task is to understand and remove everything that prevents you from experiencing love as your own basis. The more you can genuinely express that experience in life, the more love will become the focus of your identity. Thus is happiness realised; to have a fulfilled life, you have to seek your own loving nature. There is nothing selfish in this, for what you find leads you inevitably to the service of others.

(Note. Modern physics unravels the physical principles by which the universe is created. Scientists, describing and categorising forms and energies, present them as 'abstractly' as they can, denying qualities of feeling in themselves. One is not supposed to feel angry or joyful at the experience of photons, much less project such qualities upon them. The 'scientific approach' regards them only as 'photons'. Since love, the essential quality, gives *feeling* when experienced, the scientific method can never really comprehend the true nature of the universe - it has denied love 'a priori'. There is a point when physical enquiry must merge with spiritual experience for the most profound insights.)

Experiencing Love

Love is the basis of everything. Humans experience love through relationship. By consciously deciding to seek more and more love in their lives, they become aware of their own essence. Thus they approach vibrant oneness, the basis of form and the source of bliss.

A conscious decision to seek love implies an identity — a self — that can make such a choice. Babies do not have this identity. To become fully human, they have to develop one. A baby being is love, innocent and vulnerable, but without the consciousness that would enable it to know that it is love. It is the way things are. Even the instinctive life of the human baby is small. It needs *human relationship* in order to survive and to develop a sense of self which can make choices to seek love. Human relationship inexorably links it to the existing world of human consciousness.

There is no escape from culture, language or nationality — all of which are lying in wait - via parents and siblings. The baby enters this interaction equipped with the desire to live, which is expressed physiologically in its needs for food, drink and warmth. As those who provide for these needs are identified as seperate from the general environment, consciousness begins to emerge. Through this identification, the child begins to experience love in a conscious way.

What love *means* for the child is very strongly affected by the treatment which it receives from such primary figures. Since it has no other yardstick, the little child accepts the providers it loves as perfect. As they are not, its definitions of love can be distorted in the earliest stages of its development.

In extreme cases, a baby/child brought up with violence may incorporate violence into its definition of love. One brought up with parental withdrawal may bring distance into its definition of love. One brought up casually may define indifference as love. And so on. To find the way back to true love — the source of bliss — all such misidentifications must be overcome.

When a child's wishes are not immediately gratified, it experiences a sense of *frustration*. It starts to wish that things could be better arranged than they already are; it has become cognizant of a self separate from its experiences. Through separation the child can begin to *evaluate* the world around it. By the time the child begins to experience itself as a separate identity, distortions of what love means are already in place.

As childhood continues, more complex forms of expression, social rules and customs are added to basic identifications and frustrations. The little child interprets, and is changed by, its surrounding situations. Because this is the way everybody develops their individuality, people grow up with enormous confusions about the way to search for and express happiness — often passing them on to their own children. For these reasons, most people have to make a major shift in perspective to comprehend that love is the real source of happiness.

For everybody without exceptions, there are moments which could lead to the discovery of the essence — Love. These 'clues' may be ignored, rejected or misinterpreted; nevertheless, they are there. Often, they are moments which seem outside of normal — socially accepted — experience, giving them a mystical quality. Here are some examples:

• experiences where the self seems to merge with nature;
• experiences of a sense of oneness in otherwise ordinary social situations, accompanied by intense feeling;

• experiences that may occur when someone consciously seeks love, such as in meditation.

During such moments there is an 'expanded' conscious-ness; the self merges into indefinable unity. Since these experiences are beyond the scope of normal conscious-ness, they are also beyond the scope of common language, and people have great difficulty in describing and com-municating them. These special moments are short-lived and cannot be recreated at will.

Every human being has such experiences appropriate to their consciousness. They are 'extra-social' and do not arise logically out of the particular setting in which they occur. *They are a practical proof of the existence of Grace.* Love is more than the passive existence of universal oneness. It moulds itself into experiences which potentially expand and redirect consciousness. It not only *exists*, but also *man-ifests*. It can focus to support an individual.

The challenge is that not all extraordinary experi-ences are mystical. Some may be symptoms of delusion or even mental illness. You need to have discrimination and integrity to evaluate them and understand their meaning. As you make the effort, you can discover that literally everything that occurs is part of a divine drama of separation and reunion, and every experience, of what-ever kind, has a place and a function.

(Note. This focussing of love also happens when a divine teacher appears on earth to assist in the discovery that love is the source of happiness. Rather than a projection of love outward upon a form ('Love is there, but not in me!'), devotion to such a teacher may assist in the dis-covery of love within: 'He helps me to find love within me', or, 'Love manifested guides me to my own essential love'. But remember that not all love-professing teachers fully embody what they profess.)

More about Consciousness

In the highest experience, manifest creation is realised to be love and known as continuous ecstasy. This is truly Divine Consciousness: 'Being, Awareness, Bliss'. It is total human fulfilment, the soul merged in love with all creation; the Divine and the human become one, without separation.

Why is such a thing a goal, if it is already there, the essence and birthright of all humans? Why are even the 'clues' to it ephemeral and tantalising, often misinterpreted and feared as bordering on insanity? One reason is that the consciousness of the average person is not prepared for such powerful energy.

If a high amperage is put through an inadequate circuit, a fuse occurs at the weakest point. The circuit has to be strengthened before it can take the higher amperage. Love is the *energetic* basis of all creation. To experience it constantly as a reality requires both physical and mental development. This does not necessarily entail endless hours spent in meditation in silent places; since humans are capable of experiencing Divinity, they require the *practice* of love to discover its omnipresence. If one is potentially able to run a mile in, say, five minutes, one has to have the determination and physical capability to perform the task. This is achieved partly by exercises, but, above all, through *practice*.

There is another reason why enlightenment is not quite readily available. To understand it, we must return to childhood development.

Without a sense of self, consciousness cannot grow. In a little baby, this sense of self hardly exists; a nascent consciousness floats in a sea of undifferentiated, unexperienced love. The self is 'drawn out' by interaction with its particular environment, and builds up a 'personality'. The early experiences of relationship are so powerful in this developing identity since it cannot resist them. Because the sense of self is so unformed, the child's experiences have a powerful effect on its identity.

As growth continues, the child becomes more powerful, more adaptable and less overwhelmed by input. It interacts more; the self congeals. A relatively stable sense of self, the Ego, emerges.

Gradually, more or less consciously, it develops *'strategies'* for coping with the challenges posed to it and tries to resolve its problems by these means. The more effectively a strategy 'works' for a child, the more it tends to be adopted as part of the ego. *Thus, an individual illusion is created, which separates the ego self of practical short-term strategy from the potential self of limitless, joy-filled love.*

To the psychological illusions of a developing child are added social ones. In the present age, a materialistic consciousness is a strong component of almost every ego on the planet. It says: 'The way to happiness is through what you have, what you do and what value others attribute to you - prestige'. Many people hold on to this illusion until death's door — the end of the road for the soul's lifetime ego — frustrates it.

In these psychological and social ways, the ego, which is necessary to the achievement of personal consciousness, acts as a powerful block to the awareness that love is the real way of being. Thus, that which has created the self has to be surrendered for the realisation of the True Self — quite a challenge.

If ego is to be suddenly overthrown, what may remain? The fear of madness, oblivion, social ostracism, and poverty have all been advanced as good reasons for keeping within the ego's boundaries. Deep, suppressed childhood traumas may subvert even a determined wish to find love. Desires for instant gratification may make a seeker impatient and easily discouraged. The path to self-realisation requires understanding and a cool head. Small wonder then that it is not so often taken.

The established religions do not always help. In order to regulate social action among individuals living illusions about happiness, religious systems have not only taught that 'God is love, and love is God'; but their moral codes have become law and practice. This is a great dilemma for all religious teachers: God seems more 'out-side' than 'inside' and morality becomes command rather than discovery. Some religious institutions almost end up denying that there is an 'inside' — a direct connection to love — God — in each individual. Such a love link could threaten the authority of the churches organisations them-selves, not to mention that of social institutions at large. This is one of the reasons why love expresses itself in per-fect human form from time to time — in order to ensure that individual's direct contact with love itself is not forgotten.

The Divine System and the Human System.

The development of the personal identity, essential to consciousness, distorts it, to create a subjective awareness: the human system. Parallel to the human system is the Divine System, interacting with it and giving it meaning.

For human beings who do not make good progress towards Self-discovery in their lives, death would be a devastating defeat. But, just as there is a cosmic physical order by which things run, there is also a cosmic moral order. Both are governed by the law of cause and effect. The workings of the moral order have been discovered by inner exploration, primarily by the spiritual teachers of India.

A man who kills another, if discovered, is subject to the moral effect of punishment in the human system. In the 'divine system', all action has a moral effect. Some religious systems believe in the 'day of judgment' after death, when the soul is judged according to its earthly actions and allocated an appropriate place — heaven, limbo or hell (eternal damnation). But love knows no damnation. All creation is on an eternal path to conscious reunion; this is love's way of experiencing itself.

Although the individual's personality dissolves with death, the soul is clothed in the consequences of its actions. It does not die, but re-emerges in life as another being to work out those consequences and create new actions. It therefore has another opportunity to experience love and find happiness. This law of moral cause and effect is called 'karma'.

An individual soul is a non-material aspect of divine energy. It is endlessly reborn in different forms until it has developed its consciousness to the point of experiencing oneness and its truth as love. Life is an opportunity for learning about the universality, omnipresence and feeling of love. Eventually all souls learn this lesson — they are reborn continually until they do — and consciously reunite with love. There are no failures; but because of differing individual attitudes, some soul-experiences take longer than others. However, at any given moment, conscious mergence is available, if the identity is prepared to accept it.

Physical existence is not random karmic discovery. Love is not merely passive and existent. It is dynamic and supportive. The divine regulation of life ensures that every soul's experience is regulated and relevant to its choices. This grace-filled intervention operates constantly, although individuals do not become aware of it until their consciousness is awakened.

We can picture creation as a divine game. Love divides itself into physical forms (the board), structures of organisation, physical and moral (the rules), the players (individual souls), and the teacher and supporter of the game (divine Grace).

Grace, the teacher, provides appropriate experiences to which embodied souls react. The miracle of Grace is the perfect governance of all the complex interactions of embodied souls , so that each individual can make choices leading to the discovery of love. This miracle of constant creation inspires awe and humility in those who become aware of it.

The 'divine system' parallels the human system, but is far, far wider. It encompasses all forms, not just human forms. It regulates the entry of *life force* into form, the entry of *consciousness* into life force and the entry of *awareness* into consciousness, until, eventually, the soul becomes aware of itself as love, and experiences itself as love. At this point, the regulator and the regulated are one, continued physical existence is a choice and incarnation is voluntary and perfect.

Great love allows freedom. The greatest joy occurs when freedom is used to find mergence. That joy, that ecstasy is Love's self-experience, or divine self-knowledge. *There were never two, only the illusion of two.* As the illusion dissolves, Love experiences itself.

Understanding the Divine System

Theologians of all faiths have struggled with such concepts as free will, divine intervention, the existence of evil and the meaning of suffering. Unless you start from the knowledge that love alone is real and that the process of creating human consciousness masks that truth, the ground is full of pitfalls.

Much theological argument merely takes the apparent world at its face value, accepting that the experiences of our normal senses constitute truth. This is fallacy, constructed to comprehend, rationalise and attempt to control an apparently external, objective reality.

But from such ignorance flows only ignorance. Solutions to human problems of war, famine and disease are always 'just round the corner'. A new technology applied in one place causes problems somewhere else. A problem is solved in this part of the world and another emerges in that part of it. By thinking that the material world is 'really real', people think that real solutions can be found in it.

If one denies that love and grace control the illusory world experienced by the senses, explanations of that world and attempts to change things will be equally illusory. For many centuries there has been no effective change: humanity has been crippled by violence, disease and suffering. The ways they are inflicted may change, but the 'solutions' do not resolve problems — because these really stem from its alienation from love.

If the evidence of the senses is not subordinated to the practice of love, karmic cause and effect continue to operate from the divine system like a rule of a game, in order both to expose the effects of ignorance and to offer choices that could lead souls to the wisdom given by placing love first. The way to knowledge of the divine system and alignment with it is the practice of love. You can either apply love in life through service; or reject all that is 'not love' by devotion (surrender to God); or, in stillness, strip off all superficiality to become aware that love is the ultimate reality.

Love is fundamental. In different eras the relative importance of service, devotion and stillness may vary, though the practices are never exclusive. In the present 'action packed' age, service is most important.

Subtlely, little by little, the practice of love itself — and not merely its discussion — changes consciousness, expands it. It does not matter where one starts; the murderer or brute, who *chooses* not to murder or be brutish moves in love's direction. Grace and new understanding will flow to such a person in measure: 'Take one step towards Me and I will take ten towards you."

The practice of love develops a certain feeling concerning aspects of one's daily life. This 'feeling' is not emotional but intuitional — an access to wisdom. It has nothing to do with deluded states, nor is it quite the same as conscience, which is concerned with mentally internalised social moral codes.

Such intuitive wisdom leads one to the awareness of three basic principles. One, love is the basis of all things. Two, the operation of the observed world depends on a Divine system. Three, a direct inner connection to love is possible.

These principles really turn everything around. In the human system it seems that 'a dog is always a dog'. Wisdom shows that 'a dog is a dog' by Divine Grace. *If you are near the source of Grace, the dog may turn out to be something else entirely.* There is a story of the God figure, Krishna, walking with His devotee, Arjuna.

"Look, Arjuna, over there sits a crow!"
"Yes, I see the crow."
"No, Arjuna, it is a pigeon!"
"Indeed it is a pigeon."
"No, it is a sparrow!"
"Of course, it is a sparrow."
"Arjuna, you are merely agreeing with everything I say to please Me!"
"No, Krishna, You are the definer of reality. If You say it is a crow, it is a crow; if You say it is a pigeon, it is a pigeon and if a sparrow, then a sparrow it is."

This story shows that the human system — the 'objective' world — is really defined by the Divine system. It is only by love's adherence to the 'rules of the game' that the human system appears to be real and responds to the scientific 'laws' that scientists have deduced for it. The application of Grace can change or 'bend' these rules at will.

Baldly stated, the above is just information, subject to argument and discussion. But by actually practicing to love, you will come to know the reason for it in your heart, your 'innermost being', so you won't need to get into argument. Through the practice of love, intuitional feeling develops and wisdom begins to emerge in consciousness.

The practice of love is not something intellectual. Life is a school, but not an 'academic' one. People from any walk of life undertake the 'course of study' which the practice of love entails. The conscious choice to do so is the choice to take a spiritual path in life, but you can practice love and achieve wisdom without building theories about it.

As long as the ego is still powerful there are psychological pitfalls on all the paths to wisdom. Feelings towards other people are strongly coloured by qualities of the ego: sexual desire, attachment, dependency, admiration, envy, hatred, rejection and so on. Love differs from all such attitudes; rather, it is masked by them. For instance, a worker in an office may have a boss and a subordinate. Their roles may make one seem superior and the other inferior, an egoistic attitude which arises from the human system. By overcoming this attitude and respecting and valuing both colleagues, irrespective of their roles and performance, they will be moving in the direction of love.

Love is *detached* from either a role or a performance. But a general may remain detached whilst ordering the deaths of thousands, so detachment *alone* is not the essence of love.

A mother deeply loves her child, and much attachment is involved. If she extends her affection to all children, she will be moving towards love. The practice of love is always *expansive*, incorporating larger and larger categories of things.

A business man may see a wood, and view it as an opportunity for saleable timber. If he views all woods with such an opportunity in mind, he is certainly being expansive, but by no means approaches love. If he begins to see one tree in that wood as *intrinsically* beautiful, perfect, wonderful, he then begins to approach love, for he is *accepting* the tree as it is.

Love is 'coloured' by appropriate qualities, depending on the situation. Examples are: *patience* in repetitive tasks; *respect* when working with nature; *compassion* in accepting human ignorance and suffering.

The happiness that comes with love may bring tears to the eyes in its intensity. But someone who enjoys spanking so much that it brings tears to their eyes is not practising love. Qualities attributed to love cannot themselves define it. Love is basic and ultimate. It is defined by its experience, and descriptions are never quite adequate.

People who come to know love, their essential Self, are wise. They are unaffected by the ups and downs of life in the human system. Intuitively, they know that everything derives from the Divine system. *They are full of compassion for human beings who struggle in life, unaware of their own perfection.* Those who have loving wisdom serve, not to demonstrate the practice of love, but as loving agents of Grace.

The Practice of Love as the Way to Love

The three main forms of the practice of love are service, devotion and stillness. Let us examine them further.

Service should not simply be thought of as doing good for others. There are many ways of 'doing good' that have distorted psychological motives and are fraught with illusion. For instance, if a person feels inadequate in themselves, they might feel better when caring for others who are less well off. This is not service, but projected insecurity. It is as if a person were to say to another: 'I am only 3/4 of a person. Lend me 1/4 of yourself and I'll be allright.' Such a 'server' is really being served. They need the poverty and deprivation of others to 'do good' to. What would they do without a famine, crisis or third world to provide them with fodder for their own needs? Although it is possible to find a path to love through any activity, a person who does not feel worthy without helping other is truly being served by them rather than serving.

A preliminary to true service is to make a connection with love within. *Service is to act from it.* In fact, nobody who finds love can resist serving. It is an imperative, just as water building up behind a dam will somehow find an outlet in the end, be the dam ever so high. Service comes from wholeness, not from lack. Wholeness comes from contact with love.

Before any prestigious and high-sounding activities, *the first and most basic form of service is consciously to practice looking lovingly on others.* Initially, this is an act of will; and it will instantly put you in touch with the illusions which veil love. Looking with love is like digging a little channel to let water flow out of the dam. As soon as it starts flowing, it enlarges the channel by its flow. The practice of looking with love gives a person energy and motivation to get rid of their personality blockages so that the Divine system may be more freely expressed. What an energy that releases what a motivation! Such a simple thing, such a good feeling! One is not a sinner, expiating guilt, but a human being expressing the Divine within.

Look lovingly on your room, on the clothes you have to wear, on your belongings, on the world of nature, on your partner or your children, on your friends, on your parents and relatives, on strangers, on your enemies. To practice this for even half an hour a day is the beginning of service. Think of all of them with *love*, not judgment, criticism, or qualifications — without 'buts'. You will find happiness moving into your life and out into the world. Frustration with the world which seemed to be the cause of your troubles turns towards the real cause, ego structures, and gives you the determination to reform and transcend them.

Just a little lovingness practised is the next step in service. Lovingness expresses love, and opens inner channels to wisdom, Grace and the Divine system. Through it knowledge of the Divine will become possible and you will want to follow it, knowing Love as a teacher which gives you the optimum path, blending its lessons with your desires to support Self-realisation.

Once love begins to flow, some means for action will be provided by Grace. In service, the act done is much less important than the quality with which it is done. A woman cleaning her home may provide more service to humanity than an aid worker distributing relief food packages to the starving, if the former acts with love and the latter from insecurity.

Ultimately, it is only love, increased drop by drop, that can resolve problems. It is a mistake to think of 'trouble spots' as being somewhere else, to do with another part of the planet. Like a run-down body which breaks out in a boil somewhere, so a system with little access to love will produce 'trouble' spots at some point within it. Poverty and starvation, epidemics and brutality are a direct result of lack of love in the system. A loveless person cannot find happiness; nor can a loveless humanity. There are adequate resources for everyone to enjoy a life of physical well-being — only lack of love stops them flowing appropriately. Humans struggle to solve these problems through changing social systems, but any loveless system will create problems, no matter how perfect it may seem on paper.

Again and again people are deluded by achievement. They want to see immediate results! Achievement without love is hollow: an empty form giving at most, ephemeral satisfaction. If love is not present, the 'achievement' of feeding the hungry does not resolve the problem of famine, which merely rears its head elsewhere. Of course, you do put a band aid on a cut, but it is better to deal with the carelessness which led to cuts; don't think you have achieved something great by putting on a band aid.

Service is the practice of love most easily accessible and valuable in a world starved of love. It involves surrender to grace, trust that the right lessons are being given, faith that all tasks are transient and will be changed at the appropriate moment. It is not easy to release human will and become totally aligned with divine will. But service will take you there.

The second aspect of the practice of love is *devotion*. Devotion is love surging into wonder, surrendering in the knowledge that, though seemingly separate, you are one with love. Devotion acts primarily through the *feeling* self, cleansing it, purifying it, elevating it. It also carries rationality along with it, as a surge of water carries with it all the flotsam that has been lying around.

Devotion arises in the heart, as you realise your utter minuteness compared with the overwhelming and infinite universe. It arises as a fraction of the divine order guiding all lives is revealed to you with overwhelming consciousness. Devotion bursts out when a perfect embodiment of love in human form reveals itself. It is characterised by a feeling of expansion of the heart, by awe and wonder: Love overwhelms.

Devotion to an abstract, conceptualised love is most difficult, nor is it a quicker or purer way to oneness with love — as mental pride sometimes suggests. It is a great challenge to try and deny the physical, human side of feeling in order to find transcendance. Devotion to a Divine teacher is the easy way, the holistic way through the forest of attachment and desires in the human personality.

As with other spiritual qualities, the roots of devotional attitudes lie in human relationship. A baby expresses devotion in its dependency on and trust in its nurturer. Its feelings become coloured by the way its needs, desires and demands are satisfied. People often begin a devotional relationship with a teacher by projecting onto him or her their experience of this primary relationship, looking for the flaws they once discovered in parent figures.

For devotion to be in the present, such motives have to be transcended. Divine figures on earth always suffer from projections from the past. They are rarely seen for who they are, in spite of the intensity of devotion of their followers.

Spiritual teachers come to focus love and adoration. Their task is to embody love so purely that projections from childhood have no peg to hang on. In a developing relationship of faith and trust, their role is to unveil the mystery of the Divine system and, beyond that, the perfection of love, so that the devotee can begin to experience it. Once devotion, genuine and spontaneous, begins to flow, it can be purified through prayer and song, reflection and meditation, till confusions from childhood wither away.

True spiritual teachers have penetrated illusions, discarded ego and are indifferent to all the projections showered upon them. Even if they sometimes play an 'as if' game with their devotees — 'It looks as if I am angry or neglecting you, but I am actually purifying your devotion, for love's sake' — they continue to see divinity as being equally present in all, irrespective of behaviour. Devotion to a Divine teacher makes acts of grace personal, immediate, and comforting, as the devotee's mind strives to unite with love, disentangling it from the strings of illusion.

Devotion is still not perfected, however, as long as it is directed solely at one figure. For that figure can only be an exemplary expression of the Divine. *All are equally divine, and shrouded in the cloaks of confusion.* As devotion purifies, it bubbles over into compassion for and service to all humanity and creation, love's own projections in the great game of life.

Everyone teaches each other. Nothing is more delightful than to share love with others. But *devotion* to other seekers is not proper unless one is able to love each equally without projection or attachment, thereby experiencing them as divine embodiments. If you project perfection on to someone who is not perfected, you misplace your faith and enter once more into the karmic chain of cause and effect.

Love expresses itself in being and in living. But as devotees strive towards Self-awareness, they can easily become trapped by the power of love's acts and the admi-

ration which they cause in others. Ego seeks to appropriate power and admiration, to find gratification in fame
and reputation. Once again, a new cycle of karma begins.

So remember that all acts of love belong to love
alone. As you work on Self-discovery, dedicate every 'suc-
cess', every 'achievement', every 'gift of grace' to the
Divine teacher. Let your day be full of His name, your
thoughts be full of His presence.

Do not attempt to own your acts. They are love's.
Dedicate them to love, in devotion and humility. Use your
free will to surrender your ego to love, completely and
without inhibition. Then you will find love.

Stillness and Understanding

The third aspect of the practice of love is stillness. Through it you can discover your true identity and find fulfilment. Through stillness, the mind is calmed, allowing argument and thought to drift away so that love alone is 'laid bare'.

To describe spiritual experience effectively and share it with others in a book, talk or video energises and stimulates interest in self-discovery. But there is a great distinction between scholarship, which is based on argument and learning, and an *experience* of Truth. To see a sign at a street corner which says 'Restaurant this way', does not stop your hunger. At best, it helps you to know where to eat. Using stillness as a discipline at first supplements and then supplants book learning and argument, and gradually cleans up the identity by reducing unnecessary speech, idle chatter and thoughtless words. This is a form of practising love.

Though discipline is not an end in itself, it is required to learn any skill. You cannot be a physician or carpenter, bus driver or astronaut without first subjecting yourself to discipline. Similarly, learning stillness requires it. For many people nowadays discipline has to be learned before it can be practised, which makes this method of spiritual development doubly hard. Even with discipline, seeking Love out through meditation can be very arduous. The Buddha took seven years of sitting to find it.

Although spiritual experience does not come through normal sensory channels, it carries with it a certainty that is deeper than sense-perception. Often we *think* we see, hear, and so forth, but we actually do not. But an experience of that which *is*, *as* it is, is never forgotten and leaves no room for doubt. You can doubt everything, but not the experience of love.

The aim of stillness is to free the self from attachment to sense impressions, memory, random thought and material aspiration, so that you can experience love through and through.

The process is to slough off layer after layer of the personality — 'Not this, not that' — till love alone is left and real — 'I am that'. Repetition of a holy name or of holy sounds, or contemplation of the pictures of spiritual teachers may help to still thought. Physically comfortable bodily positions give ease in the attempt.

With stillness comes a sense of detachment. After a while, this is infused by love, until a great compassion for the created world emerges. This compassion remains for a time after such a meditation, but fades if it is not repeated.

A meditating figure sits still and upright, in a solid position comfortable for the body. A chosen mantra, or a holy name, may be repeated. The eyes are closed, or, if open, focussed on objects which do not provide a stimulus — for example, a blank wall. An inner, verbal preamble may set the intention for the time in stillness. If such sitting is the sole practice, it must be prolonged and prolonged. Grace will be given to help the endeavour. As one approaches Love, wisdom about the divine plan of creation becomes available, physical limitations are removed and the soul is divinised. At the final stage, time and space are transcended, and Love alone is real. Neither sound, mantra, nor picture has any further significance.

All three ways of discovering and practising love — service, devotion and stillness — are valid paths to Love. They are not mutually exclusive. All of them benefit not just the seeker but also humanity itself.

In this epoch, the proportion of time spent in service is highest, that in contemplative stillness least; but the balance may change with age and individual circumstances. The final experience however is the same. Through practice of the three forms, you will discover which 'blend' of them is best for you. Anything that does not expand love — real happiness — in you is valueless.

The practice of love releases love's energy so that it flows through the world. Subliminally, it stimulates a desire for love in others, thereby becoming an aspect of Grace.

Judgment is Redundant!

The discovery of love profoundly changes human identity. Whilst there is no way to escape the past, which is the ladder of human growth to love, there is no necessity to linger on the lower rungs cursing past events, or feeling guilty about them. Nor do you need to have nightmares about the things that you did. They were done during many lifetimes and all human history is mirrored in your own.

In the secret corners of the past lie your deeds of ignorance and thoughtlessness. They are like sterile trails, petering out in a desert from which the only way out is to retrace your steps. Within your own past, you carry all that you might nowadays judge others for. You are different only because you have become wiser and such things no longer attract you.

Since you used to do the things for which you judge others, your judgment can only be deemed self-judgment or redundant. Evil actions are the result of love veiled by ignorance — consciousness ruled by a simple egoism which seeks immediate gratification. Since you, yourself, are the person you judge, be compassionate.

This does not mean that one should condone evil acts. It is not right for someone, even on a human level, to escape the consequences of their actions, otherwise they will be more likely to continue doing ill. Human systems of judgment are there to detect wrongdoers and those whose job it is will mete out punishment. But the Divine system runs by experiential training. Grace, in its compassion, gives the soul lessons which have the best of hope teaching that ignorant behaviour does not lead anywhere.

However, *judgment is not one of the consequences of an evil act*. Judging a person because of their actions is as inappropriate as if judging the sun for sometimes keeping behind the clouds. Evil people are quite as much divine as the righteous, in spite of the differences between their actions. They have the same potential to discover love as devotees, although their circumstances may differ. Every act has the potential to create a new step towards love consciousness.

Do not hate, revile or judge others. Have compassion for the executor of a crime, be it ever so great, as well as for its victims.

For yourself, do that which is right within the moral system of society; or better yet, unite with divine wisdom and act from it. Jesus suffered Himself to be tortured and crucified, knowing that it would open a great pathway to love for humanity. This act of love cannot be considered a happy experience in the normal sense. But if Jesus had not done it, it would have meant a devastating and inconceivable unhappiness, even greater and more prolonged than His actual suffering. If you can climb the step to love, you will know the best thing to do in life's situations — and be astonished very often. But judgment of others only puts you in chains.

Imagine a light burning in a box, kept within a cupboard in a dark room. Take away all the casings and the room will no longer be dark. Similarly, love is like a high-frequency vibration obscured by lower frequencies. Remove the latter and love remains.

While the light is hidden in the cupboard, you have to hold on to things in the darkened room in order to get around. But once the light is exposed, it is no longer necessary. As you become more loving, many things you thought you needed will have less and less interest for you.

People who have a consciousness that is deeply

obscured experience life at a base vibration. They strike discords of greed, envy, hatred, anger, violence, and brutality. As they gradually find love, the discordant frequencies are left behind.

Love overlights all lives and all behaviour, shining from within. Thus as you find the vibrations of love within you, you are not proud, judging yourself superior to your neighbours; but more and more, you will see them as essentially the same as yourself, following a comparable path to your own.

Therapy and
the Practice of Love.

L ove is. It is released in you by its use. It lifts you up, and it brings you to who you truly are. The only way to find the love that is your essence, to understand and experience happiness is to practise it.

The practice of love does not include dissembling. Love cannot flow freely if 'secret' agendas are on hand. The human ego is adaptive and resourceful. Before blooming, a flower protects its fragile blossom with a harder casing that falls off as the flower is ready to open. The human ego is like this casing, but it is identified with self and unwillingly released, even when one wishes to do so.

At first the ego resists the call to inner spiritual awakening. It may find arguments to deny the presence of the divine in humanity. Or it may align itself with those who say that humanity can only be redeemed from sin by external forces. Or it may seek hedonism and short-lived pleasures in order to 'forget' that its days are numbered.

The acknowledgement of spirit, of love *within*, is a great breakthrough for the identity: there is a greater Self, to which the ego is redundant. At this point though, the ego is still in place. Its next strategy is to try and subvert the practice of love for its own ends. It turns a loving deed into a 'good' or 'praiseworthy' deed, a deed which shows others how 'holy' the actor is. The motivation becomes pride and status. Ego tries to turn a loving act into an act of power and prestige, which demonstrates the superiority of the performer and the inferiority of the receivers. Is money given for some spiritual teaching? Then ego will seek to turn it into a lucrative source of income in order to indulge a wealthy and indolent lifestyle.

Ego is linked to the human world. It is created by it, dependent on it and its motives. It tries to preserve itself by remaining on the human level. Ego steals around love, seeking to seal off all approaches to it. But eventually, ultimately, the practice of love will lift the Self above this level and ego will be gently and lovingly released, as consciousness advances beyond it.

Humans have now become more aware of ego consciousness, with its dark, hidden basements where the unassimilable, overwhelming experiences of childhood are stored. Just as guards around a prison cost a great deal, so much human energy is expended to repress events of the past too terrible to face, events which shade the personality with fear and anxiety. Many people spend time and resources delving amongst these dark corners, attemtpting to become aware of their ulterior motives and to release some of their stored pain.

There is no harm in delving into the past — for that is what it essentially is — as long as it does not become a way of life. If you constantly refer to your past as the source of your actions, you are trapped by it as you were when it hid in your unconscious. In fact, after a certain amount of emotional release, you actually *feed* it in the mistaken belief that you are healing it. It is easy to let your own morbid curiosity shackle you to your problems.

Each of you carries the past, not only of this lifetime, but of a thousand before it. Each of you once performed most of the nasty acts of revenge, retribution, desire and terror which are repressed by your conscious mind. That is why you *can* repress them — because you have learned the lessons and risen above them. Dwelling in the past — to find the motivations and explanations of life — is a worthless exercise. As you discover that past lives have been real, it is tempting to dwell on subliminal memories of long-resolved challenges. Since they have no longer any importance, the exercise is a diversion, without spiritual value.

Love grows by the practice of love. It may sometimes be helpful to release blocked emotional charges, but the way forward is to practise love. This de-energises the past, brings you into the present — where *love is* —, makes you aware of who you are, and allows the past to rest, quietly resolved.

A man discovered in therapy that many of his actions were motivated by an ambivalent attitude toward his mother. Instead of releasing the emotional 'steam' of this discovery and moving on, he began to excuse all his acts by it, blaming his mother for every failure. His ego had found a way to cling on for a while. If he had yelled out his pain for a short while and then consciously practised being loving to his mother, he could have healed their relationship and found happiness with her.

The practice of love heals, and guides to the Self. It creates a new identity, to which the past is but a wry memory. Even if motives are mixed, it will slowly purify them. Whatever ego's strategies, they will crumble before the *conscious*, *disciplined* and *continued* practice of love. To find out who you are, live in the present. Don't waste time!

Words and Actions

Underlying creation is a great sound. From its echo, humanity forms language and turns it into a plaything, an illusion within life's illusions, weaving and regulating, proposing and exhorting. Words only give direction and stimulation; at best they act as shorthand for experience.

Most words are uttered in the service of the human system and act as expressions of ego desires such as reputation and wealth. Humans erect mountains of words to describe simple things, which they proceed to bury under them. Even a great tome about love can make love less simple and less attainable.

So let love be expressed through your words:

• Say little, so that truth is not cluttered.
• Whatever you say, seek to let God speak it.
• Speak from quietness, consciously seeking love's presence.
• Celebrate the delights and worries of human life — its pains and sorrows — with words informed by love.
• Be love speaking and you will not bind yourself to the status and power brought by manipulating words.
• Let your words to others be a signpost to your knowledge of the source of love.

If you know little, speak little. If you know more, you will speak little anyway.

Through knowing love, you will speak less but you will communicate more. Your actions, your words and your thoughts will harmonise. You will have no ulterior motives; instead you will be love's agent, the kind of person who arouses the curiosity of others, and guides them in their own search.

To find happiness, seek the love in your heart before you speak or write; be aware of the implications of your speech for the listener and remember that love communicates directly, heart to heart.

A person who treats words in this way will be 'good company', someone that makes others think, the kind of person you should seek to be with on your journey to your-Self. Such good company will support and guide you on the path. In the end, once you are filled with love, you will no longer need good company, for you are whole and able to spread light amongst others.

Be in the Present

Each human life is bound by birth and death; in between is the time to find love and practise it. Time is merely an organisational form.

Human beings have set up time to regulate their lives. Having set it up they become dominated by it, rushing and hurrying everywhere. Modern lives are run by timetables and alarm clocks. Such things are products of anxiety and, ultimately, of a sub-conscious sense of the approach of death — for death seems to cut short all uncompleted activity.

And then comes a moment of Grace, when time ceases to have meaning. There is only now, beginningless and endless. As identity creeps back in, time returns.

How can you comprehend love if you are limited by time? In the experience of love, all that is, was, or ever shall be is *now*. All universes, parallel universes and alternative universes, all realms of visible and invisible energy are one. All is perfection. Love is now, not tomorrow, next year or after death. If you seek after something, you haven't got it. Love, you do have, now, at this moment. What is required is to know it.

There is absolutely no point in hurrying towards love. The best you can do is to practise it in whatever way is appropriate. As you do so, stress and impatience begin to disappear; a sense of harmony emerges. At first, time does not cease, but as anxiety diminishes, its significance is reduced. Time becomes subjective. It may fly or it may hover. The past may seem a moment or an age, depending on your mood. The aim is to make the present moment infinite. So many people are directed away from this moment. Some ponder compulsively on the past, seeking to rearrange things that have been, to find understanding and release. Others are full of fear and worry for the future — 'What will it bring?'; 'What does it mean?'; 'How will I do?' — trying to safeguard themselves against all risks.

If you live this moment to the full, the 'problems' of the past fall away. It is the same with anxieties for the future. It is what you do now that determines your future, not how you try to safeguard yourself.

People often try to escape time by running away into dreams and fantasies about how things might be. But there is only one place to run to with open arms: to the strong, welcoming security of the love that is present within you now; there eternity lives.

All journeys in space and time are actually journeys to now — to that moment which is the same as all other moments, to that space which is the same as all other spaces; to the time and place where you know love. *Instead of hurrying to get there, concentrate on living the now. What you experience is now.*

The game of discovery unfolds, according to your position on the 'board of life'. If you know that 'now' is the only home you should become a master player, and, demonstrating love in your every move, a *contemporary being.*

You can only 'play for now' by releasing egoistic desires for worldly achievement and status; they relate to possible future states and are a source of anxiety and strife. 'Playing for now' means practising love and surrendering your control of situations to the Divine Will.

The more you run, the faster will run whatever you seek to catch. Just stop in the now and you will discover that it has not escaped you at all, but already lies waiting at your feet. As you cease to hurry, the practice of love redeems time for you, comfortably embraces your past and future and allows you to know better who you are.

Death ceases to loom menacingly.

Perform the duties which God gives you, practice love in every moment and you become 'real' and contemporary. All that seems impossible to the anxious mind becomes easy; the 'objective' world of space and time breathes love to you and the present begins to embrace eternity: it is now — not then — that I am to be found, Love itself.

Suffering and Death

The soul seeks love at any cost. It will willingly enter painful experience as a human being to enable love consciousness to develop. The soul is aware of love as the only solution to life's problems. It seeks, prays for re-entry into life, for there, and there only, can it find the way to love consciousness. The soul will re-enter life again and again, until consciousness of love pervades the human being and wisdom is discovered. This striving of the soul for love which explains the problem of suffering: human beings, mesmerised by ephemeral desires, replay every lesson until they take up the opportunities given to them to turn their desires to love. That is the soul's motivation to enter suffering humanity.

A loved one dies; a friend is crushed in an automobile accident; hundreds of thousands starve. A child is beaten to death; a battle ground is strewn with bodies; a dreadful disease causes a protracted and painful demise. Torturers pursue their vicious work. If there is grace, why do such things occur? Suffering and death are the hardest facets of the human diamond to accept; they are the most testing.

Suffering depends on attitude, among other things. When someone is cut, one person might say, 'Oh, I should have been more careful with the knife.' Another screams at the sight of the blood. The first experiences no suffering, a little pain perhaps and a lesson learned. The second imagines they are suffering and, consequently, feels it. Their pain is magnified by fears of infection and death.

If you stretch your hand into the fire, you will be burned. That is a kind of self-inflicted suffering. If your acts deny the practice of love, you will also suffer.

Compassion towards suffering is one of love's great gifts. When you express your compassion by practising love, you begin to transcend suffering. For love is not dependent on outer experience. Engage with love and you will find happiness, for happiness depends on love, rather than the ups and downs of outer life. Lovingness ameliorates the suffering of others; it heals the sick with a deep quiet joy that is an overwhelming power. By strengthening your connection with love, you learn that your suffering is the result of non-loving *action*. If you are centred in love, happiness can be present, in spite of pain, for suffering and pain are both *reactions*.

While the world is occupied by people who are motivated by material possession, the degree of suffering rises. Greed results in poverty and starvation; luxury in squalor; envy in crime; and power in violence. Those who themselves do not materially suffer (at the time), but are full of greed, cause suffering for others, even if the parties are separated by thousands of miles. *Grace provides the resources for all to live. How they are divided and used by men and women is the responsibility of humanity and reflects its moral state.*

A human society centred in love might not be materially wealthy, but it would have little or no suffering. If you can understand this you will be able to see suffering for what it is. Be compassionate to those who experience the results of not turning to love. When you feel suffering yourself, you will know that your soul is teaching you. Instantly hold fast to love and the lesson is learned; suffering will recede.

Another aspect of suffering is its connection with fear: fear of others' views; fear of unresolved problems from the past; fear of losing material standards that you expect; and, above all, fear of *death*.

Death is merely an interlude between births. The

physical body, possessions and ego sense are released. The soul exists as energy on a non-physical plane. For those bound by desires for the physical, death is a terrible event. But for those who know love and live by it, death is no great hurdle. For those approaching conscious embodiment as love, even the entry and exit are known and chosen.

See death for what it is and you will not suffer on account of the dead, but commend them to grace for their next appearance on the stage of the human drama. Make love and its practice your being and you will have neither fear of death nor lesser fears. Since you do not know the time of your death, practise love now. There is no point in wasting time in unnecessary fear.

Detachment and Engagement

A small child is tempted by its parent, who presents it a bright and cuddly object. Jackdaw-like, it grasps. At first, it gives it back quite readily, but after a while, it refuses. The concept of 'mine!' is born — so simply does a child enter life's training. The practice of love — spontaneous giving — thus begins to be masked by *holding on*.

As soon as holding on is established, *taking* emerges. But who may take? Anxiety about possession is born.

Next it is a question of *protecting* — and struggle arrives.

Out of successful struggle emerges the thought of *keeping*.

'Keeping' requires power, and power in the service of keeping soon leads to *aggression*. The pattern of human civilisation is easily established!

All too often, the 'gifts' of loving parents reinforce 'mine' and 'my-ness', with their attendant chain of dubious qualities. But a loved parent can nurture in a way which brings to dawning consciousness the sense of wonder and reverence that comes with spontaneous giving.

Even for a young child there are choices — to hold or to give, to possess or to release. All through life such choices are offered. Give freely and joyfully, and release the ephemeral satisfaction of 'having' with all its attendant fears. View even the things which you feel you need: — house, partner, whatever — as a trust, to be used for a while in the practice of giving, and not as a possession.

Holding on ties you to the material world. It may even affect giving. A thing grudgingly, resentfully or conditionally given involves fear and faintheartedness. Calculation, thought of return, or manipulation, taint the energy of both the giver and the gift.

To a person addicted to 'having' — however little they may actually have — the idea of 'giving-living' is rather terrifying. Anxieties will crowd in : 'Perhaps I'll starve!' 'Nobody will like me!' 'People will laugh at me!' 'I won't be respected!' 'I'll be vulnerable to anyone's whim!' 'Who'll look after me when I'm old!' 'If I don't cling, my partner will leave!' . . . . These are the ghosts of the human world, its terrifying phantoms, sired by holding which make release so fraught.

None of this is unconquerable. The practice of loving provides strength and joy. Every step towards love draws grace. It works! Little by little the fears can be understood for the illusions they are.

The entire material world, with all its relationships and interactions, is God's gift. Even qualities which one 'possesses' — humour, anger, fearfulness, desire and so on — are God's gifts. Love has released them into form and energy.

The real source is not the gift but the *giver*. Capture the Giver and all is yours. But the Giver is not located in the physical dimension; nor can He be reached by space-ship or through 'hyper-space', neither can He be ensnared by spells or psychic power. The Giver is Love and resides in your spiritual heart. By the practice of love and detachment from all His gifts may the Giver be found.

So do not grab at the artefacts of the Giver, be they ever so tempting. Centre your desires on the real prize, aim high!

The Giver gives; so give like the Giver! Emulate Him! The Giver is love, so practise love! Let the Giver's material gifts circulate freely.

Trust the Giver's ability to give; trust your life to it and you will receive all that you need, but continue to give to others, in love. If it seems hard, start practising little by little. However much you are distracted, return to the task.

Be *engaged* in the world, a channel for divine gifts rather than their possessor. You will discover a life of bliss, without clinging, anxiety or fear. As you do, detach yourself from everything else *harmoniously*, for harmony makes detachment and engagement real.

To reach the final goal — the essence of all these gifts — even attachment to the Giver has to be released, for if the Giver were attached, His gifts would not be given on! Quietly know who you are, abandon striving and desire. But do not pretend to have reached the goal when you have not; that is dissembling. Practice of this engagement and detachment is part of the practice of love.

A world composed of people on such a search will be very different from the world of today — dominated by people holding and its retinue, fear and aggression.

Surrender

If you understand that love is life's reality, and that grace is all pervasive, you will also realise that your reality is love, and that freedom exists when you are united with the giver of grace — Divine Will.

The development of the ego has manufactured a defensive world, full of anxiety, compulsion, insecurity, projection, and all those neuroses that psychologists enjoy theorising about. As you seek love by practising it, these masks can be released. With them go previous definitions of pleasure. Instead of attachment to this or that, you begin to find love in more and more of the human and natural world. You begin to appreciate creation in all its forms.

The practice of love creates the conditions for surrender to Truth; it frees the body's energy, allows it to become a chalice for omnipresent love, and provides liberation to bliss.

The practice of *conscious surrender* supports that process. It proposes:

• God, not self, is the doer.
• Acts are done for God, not self.
• The results of actions are God's, not self's.

In your infancy you had to 'surrender' to your parents; the experience of surrender is there. To practise conscious surrender, it helps if you have a genuine spiritual teacher; for one of the duties of such a teacher is to receive this 'intermediate' surrender, and to guide you beyond form to love itself.

Surrender to parents is followed by resistance, as

ego develops and judgment grows. The divine teacher is a perfect foil for the hidden roots of ego. He or she appears perfect, as parents once seemed, and does not possess the 'faults' which the child tried to resist. A healing process can take place; for former resistances to parents are played out in projections on to the teacher, leaving the identity free to surrender *now* and see, behind the form of the teacher, Divinity itself.

Many so-called 'spiritual teachers' are incompletely evolved. Those who are genuine will transfer attachments projected by their students onwards, to a perfected teacher. If they accept such attachments themselves, they have succumbed to their own ego and cause only disillusionment to the seeker.

The practice of surrender is devotional and comprises the following elements:

• prayer;
• chanting and singing to the Lord;
• silently repeating the Lord's name till it becomes as integral as the breath;
• dedicating all actions, throughout their duration, to God.

Such devotional practice, if it is part of the practice of love, and not a meaningless ritual, accelerates the release of ego-will and builds confidence in faith and grace. It facilitates access to Divinity and the emergence of Self from the cocoon of self.

The 'devotional path' is not in itself an easy way to Love. The combined practice of love and devotion — 'integrated devotion' — provides intense and frequent experiences of bliss, which stimulates desire for love. Surrender to love — it is the perfect guide to yourself — it will never let you down.

Omnipotence and

its Attractiveness to Ego

L ove — oneness — divides itself into many; in this way, it can know itself. This initial and ongoing creative act is the acme of power. Creation and modification of physical form continue all the time, organised by physical and moral laws which also structure consciousness.

The energy of Divine Will maintains the stability and character of the entire creation. There are creative, maintaining and transforming aspects of the power of love, while the power of grace supports the strivings of consciousness towards love, bending or breaking laws governing the material world if necessary.

Such power is an attribute of Love manifest. As you seek love in yourself, you gradually begin to experience the power of Divinity in yourself.

At first, the world seems objective and rational, as obeying the laws by which it is governed. With each step towards love, this 'rationality' becomes relative. 'Coincidences' begin to multiply, leaving the 'rational' faculty of the mind, developed for a lawful world, perplexed.

It seems impossible to count on these 'coincidences: sometimes they happen, sometimes they don't. You meet a person you were thinking about. A book opens at an appropriate page. Help comes just when it is needed. An accident that seems certain is avoided. Yet accidents do occur; sometimes help does not come. This is a new subjectivity that seems capricious.

As you dedicate yourself more and more to the practice of love, nearing the source of grace, you find your thoughts and desires empowered. 'Extra' faculties emerge. The body now becomes a vehicle which may be left and re-entered. 'Impossible' things such as bi-location, the re-arrangement of the physical world, the replay of a sequence of time, direct knowledge of others' thoughts and feelings — all become possible. At a later stage, conscious control of incarnation and non-incarnation is achieved — the mastery over birth and death.

These powers have been described by Indian spiritual teachers and collectively termed 'Siddhic'. But they are known to spiritual teachers all over the world and rightly regarded with great ambivalence, a gift and a challenge at the same time.

The difficulty is that they emerge in partial form before ego has vanished from the identity. The remaining ego may give itself a boost by using elements of such powers for self-aggrandisement and prestige, or in attempts to coerce or manipulate others. Such misuse constitutes an 'abuse of trust'. If it is not corrected, it leads very rapidly away from love — like going down a snake in a 'snakes and ladders' game. And since to lose what you have almost known is a real tragedy, the exercise of Siddhic powers should be regarded with extreme caution by the unperfected seeker of Self.

Power without love causes much unhappiness. As such powers manifest themselves in you, continue resolutely with your surrender to love! *Remember that they are not 'your' power, but love's — used solely and appropriately by love, for love, and out of love.* Ultimately, when you are love, consciously and perfectly embodied, love's power will flow from you as a stream of compassionate grace, in just the right measure to each seeker.

A new age of spirituality is succeeding the age of materialism. As humans are transformed for it, the 'objectivity' of the material world will more and more be brought into question. The greatest temptations will not arise from the material per se, but will lie in the ego's attempts to manipulate Siddhic powers. Prepare yourself well, for the transition will be swift!

Humanity is Ruled by Divine Will

Humans think that their systems make the world better. People almost always say their century is better to live in than the one before. Never has it been so loudly insisted upon than in the age of materialism.

As proof of the virtue of this age over any other, people extol running water, the motor car, television, and the aeroplane, in spite of war, famine, poverty, and homelessness. Although great resources have been spent on medical care in many countries, diseases have multiplied to keep up with them.

The production of a plethora of material objects has replaced spirit as the focus of human fervour and endeavour. Since all these material things give only illusory and ephemeral pleasure, this age might be said to be the most poverty-stricken of all. Desires are stimulated endlessly and possession anxieties thrive. Commodities may become more complex, more may be known about the laws regulating the physical universe, but this is no progress if human consciousness is more and more turned away from the divine.

Love is scarce in this age; what there is, is very precious. Even a little love will secure divine grace. In this sense, the darker the age, the easier the path to spirit as love welcomes those who have turned from such manifest and multiple illusions towards the truth.

Humans think that the things they achieve and the civilisations they build are permanent; they constantly ignore their own history. Whatever the quality of past civilisations, spiritual or material, they have faded or been destroyed. For remember that all the human material resources that can be mustered — even in this age — are infinitesimal in relation to the natural powers of the universe. Only divine grace keeps a civilisation in being for a time. Divine grace, not human will, changes it.

But ego sees itself as the 'doer' and for support expands this view to humanity as a whole. It disregards the fact that love is the true doer. It operates to create, maintain and transform, as much in collective human affairs as in other parts of nature.

It is better to see humankind as actors on the stage, playing the drama of love lost and regained. Divine Grace, not humanity, structures the different settings. In every age, and in every civilisation, the theme of the drama is the same. Only the context differs. Contemporary society and civilisation are merely settings against which this universal drama is played out. God is the author, awareness of the truth of love the theme.

In this divine drama, there are four recurring epochs in human history, defined by the degree of human separation from Truth:

• In the 'great' age, humanity is close to spirit, but grace is given only as a result of extreme effort. Ignorance and wisdom are rather separate.
• In the second age, spirit is still primary, but many find themselves torn between two paths and powerful 'enemies' of spirit emerge, to try human motivation.
• In the third age, spirit and delusion are almost evenly matched, with ceaseless wars between their representatives. Even the good must conquer materialistic desires.
• And in the fourth age, materialism is dominant in almost everyone and each must wage an internal struggle to discover the truth hidden behind illusion.

It is divine power that changes these settings. At present a figure of true love is embodied on earth to usher out the age of materialism and introduce an age of spirit. The cycle is in process. It is simply the way things are, like a natural law.

The transformation takes place through all who seek love as the truth of their lives. As they follow this impulse, they begin to find their own truth. And as Grace works through them, they become agents for change. A very different human society is emerging, one which will surprise even those who yearn for it, for they also are steeped in materialistic concepts of human well-being.

One age is not 'better' than another. In each, humans struggle to attain love, learning what blocks and what facilitates their task. Nor is the task easier in one age than another. A different context brings about different practice, and presents different challenges — but the goal remains the same.

Human happiness will not be achieved by a new age, but by the discovery of love, and mergence with it. Seek that as transformations unfold about you, and you will be in harmony with them:

• Practice love in compassionate and dedicated service and you will find love multiplies.
• Surrender to the Divine will, which is the only will.
• Though engaged with the world, achieve detachment from its material things, dissolving your egoistic self so your real Self can be found.
• Wonder at transformations in the world of humanity and nature and use them to reinforce your faith.

These are the great tasks of your lives. Achieve them and happiness will be found; your lives will be well lived.

Working Together

Exercises for ' Self-Help ' Spiritual Groups

Contents

Introduction

The exercises described here are not difficult. If the instructions are followed carefully, they should not give rise to any problems. They are group exercises, because a group of people working together to find love generates wonderful feelings and a great deal of transformative power. The energy it gives off benefits the planet.

• Meet regularly

Get together with a group of your friends and have a regular meeting, every week or fortnight. You will achieve the best results if you follow the exercises roughly in the order in which they are given, but some of them need frequent repetition. The real value of the exercises emerges when you start putting some of their principles into practice in your daily life. That is a way of practising love.

• Love is the aim

Nowadays, some people become involved in many therapy-oriented groups. They think things are only 'successful' if there are loud explosion of emotion, which, after a while, they learn to manufacture. The aim of these exercises is to find and practise love, your Essence. Emotion will arise during the work, but is not its aim.

• **Meditate first**

All the exercises involve a guided meditation at the beginning and another one at the end. Do take these seriously. They aren't at all a meaningless ritual; they set the energy from which the work is performed and help to lift you from your everyday state, whatever that may be, towards love, the truth of who you are.

• **Select a group leader**

Somebody will need to lead these meditations and organise the energies in your group. Rather than being 'democratic' and trying to do this collectively, it is better to give one person the task for a whole evening. It's fine to discuss together what you'll do next week, but one person should be responsible. Don't leave anyone out; the task will help them to develop confidence in working with others,a most valuable skill. Divinity has no place for doubt or hesitation because it is all loving and all knowing. You have to practice your divinity and this means learning self-confidence. Of course, some people take much more easily to leading groups than others. If someone is finding it difficult and 'you know better', it's a good exercise for you to restrain yourself and be patient — another valuable quality to learn.

• **Share**

After each exercise, share what went on quite intensively with your partner or partners. This involves learning to take seriously all the nuances of feeling you experienced and all the images you received. Do not allow yourself to regard them as trivial. The 'bull's eye' might be hidden in your impressions. Share ideas and impressions that arise about others in the group in a supportive way. Judgment, criticism and gossip, however, are worse than valueless.

• Be disciplined

If you feel the need to talk about all that's happened to you since the group last met, separate that from the group work itself. Why not be disciplined, and start your meeting with a spiritual sharing instead? What has recently come up for each of you that might help you on your path to love? It is not selfish to share your problems and successes in coming closer to love. Not only may you be given support, but you may give help to others by sharing. To seek Self is never selfish; but to preen self is selfish indeed.

• Give loving attention

Try very hard to pay loving attention to what others are saying, even if you privately think it balderdash. That way you will learn tolerance and begin to realise that everyone has their own way of expressing themselves; you will also learn that your way or pace is not necessarily best for them.

• Have attunements

Finally, start and end any time together with an attunement or meditation. It sanctifies your time, brings you fully present when you start, and helps you to assimilate what you have learned at the end.

•Get the atmosphere right

You will need a warm and comfortable room. It's much harder to do this work if your body feels uncomfortable. Personally, I like to work on the floor, with a lot of cushions and blankets, but it's also fine to use upright chairs. Sofas and armchairs are definitely *not* recommended since you need to be as alert as possible, and not half asleep! Meditation cushions, or 'zafu's are very appropriate; see the exercise on Zen. You'll also need candles. Some people like incense, but check first; a few are disturbed by it. Also, it is a good idea to provide plenty of paper handkerchiefs. Finally, why not have fun? God is the great joker; heavy, hyper-serious efforts will soon lead to pretention — a sure way back to egotism. You can be serious *and* light.

So here we go!

Exercise 1

Starting and Finishing

This is a guided attunement to start and close a group. (Of course, you've already selected someone to lead the evening's work and the person has done their homework and prepared these meditations.)

The group leader lights a candle as a point of focus. The group, unshod, stands or sits in a circle, holding hands. Some people like to join hands with left palm down and right one up. Or you can do it with the right palm down and the left one up. It makes for harmony to adopt one way or the other and keep to it. Taking your shoes off is a gesture of respect; and it introduces a feeling of 'specialness' because the day's dirt is not brought in with you.

Here are some 'model' phrases. As with other guided meditations in these exercises, try to find your own way of putting them. If you are nervous, use these for now. Later your own way of doing it will carry more conviction.

Let's close our eyes and become still . . . (Pause)
Feel the hands holding yours, let them support you . . .
Now visualise, or sense, an inner light at the centre of the circle, the light of love and wisdom. Its source is above you, but let it spread till the whole circle is filled with it. . .
Now, let it enter you and fill you , until you and all in the circle are glowing in the light . . .
We ask for blessing for the work we shall do this evening/ today . . .

*May everything come from the light and be in the light,
from the highest source, for the entire time we are working
together . . .
We give thanks that it will be so . . .
Now, gently open your eyes and spend a moment looking
at each member of the group in welcome . . .
Thank you.*

To close the group after a session, hold hands again.
The group leader says (model words):

*Let's close our eyes . . .
Let's take a moment to think of all that's happened in the
group tonight . . .
We give thanks for all we have received . . .
Let's feel the hands holding ours, and accept love and
support through them . . .
In turn let's give love and support to the two people
holding **our** hands . . .
We ask for blessing on this group and its continued work . . .
Thank you.*

The group leader squeezes hands as a sign to finish
and everyone else follows in turn, so the squeeze is passed
round the circle.

Points to note

Silence is as powerful as words. Don't rush things
but use the pauses to leave time for silence. On the other
hand, don't drag, or people's minds will start to wander.
It is crucial to emphasise working with the 'light' of love
and wisdom; it needs to be reiterated before each exercise. Establish in your mind that you'll be in this 'special
state' for the whole period involved, be it an exercise or
an evening's work.

(Why not begin to invoke love at the beginning of
your day — and night — too? It will keep you attuned to

the best you can attain and lift you to even better!)

Right after the opening attunement is a good time for introductions (if there are new members in the group) or for a brief sharing .

Whatever you are doing, the opening attunement should, without fail, precede your time together. The aim of such groups is spiritual development, not curiosity or 'personal growth'. Spiritual development is, in fact, by far the easiest way to 'personal growth'.

Exercise 2

Looking with Love

Many teachers use a variant of this exercise because it is so important. I have found this way of doing it to be very powerful. Its effectiveness depends a little on the way it is introduced by the group leader, so the form of words is quite important.

The group is divided into pairs. (If some people don't yet know each other, encourage them to work with someone they don't know.) Each pair should keep as far apart from the other pairs as the room will permit, but they themselves should face each other and be as close together as they can comfortably be. Don't let people get away with sitting a metre apart; chivvy them closer, up to, but not over, their point of embarrassment.

Make sure that there is no talking during this exercise. It ruins the energy.

Partners must decide who is 'A' and who is 'B' before the exercise starts.

Here are some model words for the group leader:

Close your eyes, everyone become still, just with yourself . . .
We ask for blessing on this little exercise, . . .
for everything to be in and from the light . . .
Now, visualise your partner as far as you can.' (If the group are strangers) 'Can you remember their name? Don't worry if you can't . . .
Now, open your eyes, and A look into the eyes of B. B, allow yourself to be looked at, holding eye contact.

The next words are said very slowly and clearly, with marked pauses:

I see you . . .
*I see you **as you are** . . .*
*I see **all of you** . . .*
*I see you **without judgment** . . .*
*I see you **with unconditional love** . . .*
If you are B, open yourself as much as you can to be seen. Have you ever been seen this way before, without judgment, with a love that doesn't want anything from you? Notice any feelings you have. Can you trust this person?

Slowly repeat from 'I see you' to 'I see you with unconditional love'. If you are confident, you can say:

This is the way Jesus and the Buddha looked at people, with love for its own sake.

After some time of looking at each other in silence, you say:

Now close your eyes and be with yourself again . . . Have any feelings come up, any impressions? . . . How was it to see or to be seen for you?

Leave a little time for self-reflection, then continue:

Now open your eyes again. This time, B, look into the eyes of A. A, open yourself to be seen.

Repeat the rest of the words as before, with pauses. Don't shorten it or lose emphasis. After a similar time, you say:

Now close your eyes again and go inside . . .
Notice anything at all that comes up for you . . .
Is there a difference between 'seeing' and 'being seen'?

Give a pause for silent reflection . . . Then:

Now open your eyes again, thank your partner and share with them what you experienced.

Allow plenty of sharing time, but not so much that people start talking about the weather! Then bring the group together and see if there are experiences the whole group can share. This encourages togetherness and different perspectives.

Looking with Love in the Whole Group

The group stands in a circle with eyes closed. The group leader asks the members to open their eyes and slowly look at everyone in the circle with unconditional love. Then eyes are closed again for a short time to register the experience. It can be very moving.

Notes

This little exercise is really one of the most valuable of all. Of course, it is an artificial situation, but it introduces the idea that how you look at people is an act of volition; it can be under your conscious control. It can also be practised outside the group situation. All you need for enlightenment, is to look at everyone, everywhere, with unconditional love, all the time. So why not use the exercise as a starting point and practise it in your daily life? Soon you will realise that how you look at people is under your control. Even if it seems artificial at first, keep on! You are 'lifting' your own energy by doing it.

What is 'unconditional love'? It is not judging someone, nor expecting anything of them, but giving them compassionate attention. It is not indifference, nor the 'rational objectivity' of a scientist, for it involves feeling. Nor is it sloppy sentiment, but very calm. Words aside, everybody knows what it is, for they looked in that way at those close to them when they were babies, no matter how much they were 'disillusioned' afterwards.

In this exercise, being looked at involves surrender. All the defence systems we have will shout 'caution'. But, if somebody looks at you with unconditional love, there is no need for defence. For beneath all their problems and difficulties, illusions and confusions, everybody actually does look at you with unconditional love. If you can ignore all that is superficial, you are being seen by God and there is no need for defence. You can be confident and clear even though you are defenceless. That is freedom!

Naturally, people's reactions to this exercise vary. Some find it hard; some frightening; some may cry. It is good to notice all these reactions and talk about them, without judging them as 'trivial' or 'embarrassing'. Sharing is so important in all these exercises because it is a training in self-awareness. Watching oneself implies a viewer separate from the viewed. As long as judgement is taken away, that viewer is Love. Sharing helps to establish this sense of an observer in you, one apart from your personality. Gradually, you can become that loving observer and let the old identity go. That is happiness. Practise!

The task of the group leader — apart from speaking the words with conviction — is to keep aware of what is happening in the room. If people look away, quietly bring their eyes back to their partner's. If they cry, give them a paper handkerchief. If they start to talk, quietly stop them. You may be nervous at first, but try to trust God, remembering that during the meditation, you've put yourself in divine hands. God will not let you down. It's a wonderful experience to feel the energy in the room change as the group members invoke unconditional love.

Exercise 3

Challenging Negative Speech

Sun Bear, the American Indian teacher, first introduced me to this kind of exercise, also commonly used in workshops. The version used here is amended and expanded as a spiritual exercise.

The main purpose of the exercise is to increase your awareness of the 'tone colour' of your normal speech, enabling you to change it consciously. It also encourages you to let go of rational control — just a little bit —, and might give you some information about your self-image, so that that too may be open to change.

The three parts of the exercise can be done one after the other or separately. If done separately, an opening meditation is necessary for each part, and the group needs to pair off again. Eye contact with the partner should be maintained throughout.

Part 1

Having sorted the group into pairs, each with an 'A' and a 'B', and encouraged each pair to take the maximum space the room allows, the group leader proceeds as follows:

Close your eyes, sit upright and get comfortable . . .
When you open them, one of you is going to talk for five minutes to the other. The other will listen carefully without interruption or commentary. The idea is just to talk without thinking, keeping the flow going for the whole

time, if possible . . .
Now, let's bless the work . . .
May all this time together be blessed . . .
We ask that everything be from the highest, for the highest good . . .
Make a loving connection with your partner, one without judgement, a connection from the heart . . .
Now, open your eyes and look at each other and I'll tell you more . . .
B, I want you to talk about your partner for five minutes. You can say anything you like, anything at all. It doesn't even have to be true; give your imagination free rein . . .
The only condition is that there should be nothing negative or critical. As for you, A, listen carefully. Five minutes from . . . . now!

I have used the Bs to start the exercise, because the As would usually expect to begin, and have 'prepared themselves', but take your pick.

After five minutes:

Time's up. Both of you close your eyes without talking . . .
How was it for you? Could you keep the flow going? . . .
Was it hard not to be critical? Did you succeed? . . .
A, could you listen carefully? . . .
Now, open your eyes again. This time, A will speak in the same way for five minutes about B and B listens. Once again, anything is OK as long as it's not negative or critical. Five minutes from . . . . now!

Follow the same procedure , with quiet reflection on what has happened. If you stop here, the partners may share their experiences, but it's good to go straight on — with no talking at all — to part 2, as follows:

Part 2

Same partners, same position, eyes closed.

Group leader:

Get settled once more, relax . . .
This time, B is going to talk to A and A will listen as before.
But this time, B will talk about **themselves** *. . .*
Remember, nothing critical or negative . . .
Now open your eyes and off you go, B, for five minutes.

The exercise progresses as in Part 1, giving time for reflection with eyes closed after the five minutes, after which the partners swap roles.

Now go on part 3; if you are continuing directly from part 2, no talking should be allowed.

Part 3

Same partners, same position, eyes closed.
Group leader:

This time you only have two minutes, B, to speak critically about yourself. Listen hard, A! . . .
Now, open your eyes and off you go!

After two minutes:

That's enough! Now, A, I want you to find the positive side of those critical things B said about themselves, and see if you can transform them to make B hopeful. Just listen, B, no discussion.

After two or three minutes:

Both partners, close your eyes again . . . Now it's the As' turn. Two minutes of speaking about yourself critically with B listening hard. Open your eyes and start now!

Once again, after two minutes, the As are stopped and the Bs look for the positive in what they have said.

Now a final period with closed eyes:

Spend a few minutes reflecting on the three parts of this

exercise and how you felt during each of them . . .
Remember not to judge yourself; just notice things . . .
Now, open your eyes, thank your partner and share what
happened for you.

Allow plenty of time for sharing, then some time
for the whole group to come together and share.

Notes

Most people don't have too much trouble with this
exercise but it can be hard if you have a negative self-
image or are very judgmental of others. As with the previous exercise, you can 'practise live' in everyday life,
using the exercise to help make you aware of how you
speak about others and yourself, consciously determin-
ing to be less critical and judgmental, and more supportive in your comments. It neither supports you nor others to 'play along' with negativity because it creates a
downward spiral of depressive energy.

Learning to let go and 'just speak', after meditation
is a first step in opening to intuition, itself the key to the
door of wisdom .

The exercise can be treated in a fairly light way, as
an 'ice breaker' — helping people to get to know each
other better.

For the Group Leader

Your job has both inner and outer aspects. On the
outer, you are 'keeping the players playing according to
the rules', encouraging them to continue if they stop, and
halting chatter between the parts. You speak clearly and
slowly, giving enough pauses for inner reflection.

But you are also 'holding the energy' in the room,
observing what is going on carefully, reaching out with
love to everyone. Sometimes you go over quietly to anyone who is stuck and just stand near them. Often, doing

this is enough to free them to continue. Don't worry too much if someone is struggling for things to say. This may be a necessary step towards self-awareness, allowing them to identify what they need to change in themselves.

Don't get worried if someone cries a little; give them a hanky! If someone gets quite upset, you can put a hand on their shoulder and encourage their partner to hold their hands if they want that.

But always keep part of your attention with the rest of the group, 'holding the energy' for the whole room.

Don't forget to keep the time!

Don't feel worried by any situation that might come up. You won't be given anything that you can't handle. Thank you, God!

Exercise 4

Becoming the Light — a Guided Meditation

Sai Baba recommends this as a regular meditation for individuals. However, it is easy to adapt for a group. It uses your imagination to help you connect with your reality, and symbolises the three stages of the spiritual path: dualism, where God is seen as separate from you; qualified monism, where you seem a differentiated part of God; and monism, where you are pure divinity, having attained full truth. At this final stage you are free, perfect and the source of light itself.

In the group, this meditation can be done with soft background music, which enhances the atmosphere. Use contemplative, spiritual music. Try it first without music and then repeat with the music.

The group sits in a circle, facing a candle placed in the centre. The group leader then leads the following meditation. As in previous exercises, the following are 'model' words. The pauses are long.

> *Make yourselves comfortable, and breathe deeply and slowly, in . . . and out, in . . . and out . . .*
> *Concentrate on the flame of the candle, a source of light . . .*
> ***I see the light . . .***
> *Now, close your eyes and imagine that this light is in you, an inner flame . . .*
> *If it's hard, reopen your eyes and focus on the candle flame once more. Then try again . . .*

The flame can be anywhere in you, it doesn't matter where: in your head; in your heart; in your belly; anywhere . . .
The light is in me . . .
Now, imagine the light expanding till it fills you totally, there isn't any part of you that isn't filled by the light . . .
I am the light . . .
Now, imagine that, like the candle, you are giving light to the room . . .
The light shines from me . . .
Open your eyes and look at the candle again. Light is the great symbol for purity; where light is, there can be no darkness. In the light, Truth is revealed . . .
I see the light. I see Truth . . .
Now, close your eyes . . .
Imagine the light in you once again . . .
The light is in me. Truth is in me . . .
And now, expand the light to fill you completely . . .
I am the light. I am Truth . . .
Imagine the light shining . . .
The light shines from me. I spread the Truth . . .
Open your eyes again and look at the candle once more . . .
If you know the Truth, you realise that Love is the underlying reality of the Universe. Look at the flame again . . .
I see the light. I see love . . .
Close your eyes and visualise the light in you . . .
The light is in me. Love is in me . . .
And now, expand the light until it fills you . . .
I am the light. I am Love . . .
Be aware of the light shining . . .
The light shines from me. I give Love to the world . . .
Now, open your eyes once more.

At this point, a sharing can take place as to how the group members experienced this meditation. But another piece may be added — in which case, instead of saying: 'Open your eyes', you can say:

Imagine you are over (a war zone or problem area in the world) . . .

Let your light shine on this place, give Love to this place, so that people may see another way . . .

Then finish the meditation.

Notes

It is interesting to note that a candle flame is not like a material object. If you give away a material possession, you won't have it any more. But if you put something in the flame, it will also burst into flame, without diminishing the original flame in the least. Love is like the flame, not like a material thing. However much of it you give, it will still remain with you.

Indeed, Love is more than the flame. It actually expands with use. So the more you give, the more you have. This is the practice of love and the path to your own Divinity.

At first, the candle flame helps to put you in touch with your essential Divinity. Then, soon, you will be able to imagine yourself filled with light, without a candle. The final step is to know that you embody the light (Love) *in reality*. At this point, imagination or visualisation are redundant. You will *know* when you have achieved it; if you want to know *how* it is, study the life of Jesus, the realised Buddha, or Sai Baba. Love alone becomes the well-spring of action.

For the Leader

The **highlighted words** are spoken slowly with emphasis. Bathe in the beauty that enters the room as the group engages in this meditation.

Note on 'Imagination'

Most children are encouraged to use their imagination. Stories of magical events are offered to us to 'believe'. In Britain, the story of Father Christmas filling the stockings with gifts on Christmas Eve is played out for many children.

As we grow a little older, cold reason steps in as the master, and imagination is displaced. But the world of 'imagination' has a complex connection with the world of 'reality'; carefully controlled visualisation — or 'sensing' — interacts with the 'real' world, to modify or to change it. Instead of assuming that the impressions of our normal senses are 'real' and those of our imaginary fantasy worlds 'unreal', it is better to see them as being merely different, not totally separate. Each is a reflection of truth, but not truth itself; and each can be used to help us become aware of truth, or, on the other hand, to multiply confusion.

Some people have a visual imagination; they 'see' pictures. Others 'sense' or 'feel' and, sometimes, people 'hear'. All these experiences are equally valid in terms of practising imagination. So it doesn't matter if someone says, 'now visualise a leg' and you can't see it! Just sense it instead.

If you do this sort of exercise often, your imagination will increase in power. Always remember that you are its controller, not it yours. Never believe the classical fallacy that the world of the senses is real and that of imagination unreal. Both are unreal. You use them to find reality, that is, Love.

Exercise 5

A Game
with Sai Baba Cards

A group of Sai devotees in Glastonbury has produced a set of over 300 cards, each with a saying from Sai Baba on it. These beautiful cards are available from esoteric bookshops. In this exercise, we demonstrate the presence of Grace, working through 'chance', and work playfully with our intuition. The exercise is in two parts, which should be separated by a little break. Each person needs a pen and some paper.

Part 1

The cards are laid out face down on the floor. The best way is to lay them close together in a spiral, starting from a candle in the middle. The group is in a circle on the outside, facing the candle. Then the group leader leads a meditation (model words):

> *Let's all sit comfortably upright . . .*
> *Close your eyes and take some deep, slow breaths . . .*
> *Visualise a light in the centre of the circle. It spreads and fills us, so the circle shines and is united in the light . . .*
> *We pray and invoke that Sai Baba be with us in the circle, that all comes from Him, so we each may take the card most appropriate for us right now . . .*
> *Now, in your own time, open your eyes and let your hand take whichever card it is drawn to.*

When everyone has taken a card, the contents can be shared, and each person can venture comments on the relevance of their card, if they can see one. Other people can also comment on these comments, but not so a general discussion ensues. Everyone writes down the words on their card and it is returned to the pack. A moment is finally spent in silence to give thanks for the gifts received.

Part 2

The group pairs off. Each pair finds its own space and decides who is A, and who is B. Everyone has at hand the aphorism which they picked from the Sai Baba cards.

The group leader acts mostly as the time keeper in this exercise. He or she starts as follows:

> *Is everybody ready? Then close your eyes and take some calming breaths . . .*
> *Feel a light, joining you and your partner . . .*
> *Make a connection of non-judgment and unconditional love with them . . .*
> *We ask that this work comes from the highest, from the light and that the highest good be served by it . . .*
> *Now, open your eyes and A, show B the message you received from Sai Baba. When you have really understood the message, B, place yourself behind A, put your hands on A's shoulders, close your eyes and wait.*

When all the Bs are behind all the As — this is done so that all can start at the same time (a big help in building harmonious energy in the room) — the group leader continues:

> *Now, B, tell A a story which illustrates the meaning of their card. You've got ten minutes for it. Allow yourself to start with any idea that comes into your head and don't worry about how it's going to finish. It will all work out. You have ten minutes to tell the story. As, please listen carefully.*

The group leader times the exercise. After ten minutes, he or she says:

Now finish off what you're saying. Both As and Bs, close your eyes and be silent . . .
Now, open your eyes.

The partners then change roles, and the procedure continues as before, with the Bs showing their card to the As and so on. When all is finished, the group leader says:

Now thank your partner and share anything you want to about the stories.

After a reasonable time, bring the group together, so that a sharing can take place in the whole group.

Notes

All great religious teachers use parables and stories to illustrate their spiritual dicta. They enlist imagination, feeling and humour as 'digestive aids' for what is being said. Great spiritual truths are hard to describe directly in words; by parable, story or analogy, they have meaning in common experience.

In the second part of this exercise, a deeper insight into the meaning of the saying on the card may be given, but the main purpose is to practise intuitive thought. If the exercise is set up as described, the story tellers won't have time to 'think out' a story; they are encouraged to 'let go' and allow their stories to unfold from whatever idea comes to them. The tone is set by the blessing.

On the spiritual path, we are seeking wisdom. We have to overcome the belief that rationality is the source of spiritual wisdom. Since our educational system trains us to be as rational as we can in order to slot us into routine jobs, our creative intuition is usually suppressed and ridiculed. My daughter, at the age of five, was a superb poet, using words quite intuitively. After four years of school, she was reduced to turning out standard rhymes.

But if we meditate first seeking blessing and the highest — the preamble of all the exercises in this book — we will find, to our initial surprise, that *Grace will be given* and that our intuition will come up with exactly what is needed in any situation. The challenge is to dethrone reason, which is often like an inner doubt, saying such things: 'You can't without me' 'That's nonsense!' 'How do you know that's relevant?' 'You couldn't dare to risk saying that!' 'That doesn't follow' Etc . . . . But when unconditional love and non-judgment are invoked, blessing is asked, and all is done in the light of Divine Love, intuition will lead you beyond yourself towards the source of Love and happiness.

All the following exercises, with the exception of Zen, which is explained separately, involve two parts. One 'sets the energy', as described above. The other allows the intuition to flow from it. Gradually, you will become more confident in using intuition. Ultimately, Divinely inspired intuition will guide your life, and you will trust it more and more. At first, there are bound to be conflicts with rationality, which being linked to the ego, is reluctant to serve rather than to be served.

But now to Zen meditation, which will provide a deeper background to all the work.

Exercise 6

Zen Meditation

Zen is actually a variety of Japanese Buddhism, its most puritan form. Here, only an aspect of the meditation technique is introduced. The aim of the meditation is to be fully present, completely aware, but unattached. You choose a simple thing to do, 'just sitting', and make an affirmation to do that and that only.

Since you are sitting for a relatively long time, a good physical position is essential. I recommend half an hour to begin with, rising to whatever limit the group can take (about 45 minutes is probably maximum for bodily comfort without movement). You are not in search of visions or messages, just sitting; so you keep your eyes open, facing the simplest surface possible, preferably a blank, off-white wall, but whatever is available will do.

In practice, as soon as you begin to sit, you are beset with several groups of 'enemies', all intent on stealing your attention. First come the cohorts of sense impressions. How interesting, how varied a blank wall can be! What fascinating sounds can emerge in a quiet room! What after-tastes your previous meal can provide.

The next brigade come from the body. What a terrible itch! It demands to be scratched. How essential that the hair be pushed back! What agonies of pain in the joints! How the eyes want to close for just a little doze!

Then come the regiments of thoughts and feelings, from the most trivial to the most profound. And the whole army must be dealt with non-violently!

In the end, attention can always win. You may *have*

sense impressions, but you are not them. You *have* a body, but you are not your body. You *have* thoughts and feelings, but you are not them. Each time these various 'gangsters' attack, simply be aware of them, but do not respond to their demands. Keep your eyes open and keep on sitting! Let thoughts drift by, like clouds in the sky. Don't follow them, or give them your energy; they will disperse. If you remember your poor mother and how badly you treated her, or she you, let the tears trickle down your cheeks; but keep on sitting!

As you can see, Zen is an enormously powerful meditation, for, just by being fully aware and doing only that which you have set out to do — just sitting — you will become real, while all your accoutrements become illusory. It requires you to be Yourself, Divinity, sitting, for half an hour. And, with practice, it will work, even if you can't believe it at first.

There are three sitting positions, discovered from long experience to be the most helpful for 'just sitting'. If you sit on a chair, it should be an upright one with a firm seat. No easy chairs, please. You sit on the *front* of the chair, *not* leaning against the back, so that your back is self-supporting and *straight*. Your legs are apart and the feet firmly on the ground in front of you. The part from hip to knee should have a slight downward slope. If you are tall, you can achieve this with an extra cushion on the seat. If you are short-legged, you may need a folded blanket on the floor to give your feet support. If you are too far back in the chair, its front will press on the blood vessels in your leg, causing discomfort. If you lean against the back, you will drift off to sleep.

For the second position, you kneel on the floor, knees apart, using a meditation stool or high cushion under your backside. If the stool is at the right height, you will make a nice triangle, with the knees and backside as the three corners. The weight is well distributed, with your back, of course, quite straight.

The third position is to sit on a cushion and cross your legs below the knees in front of you. The knees should be *on the floor*, not lifted, which means you will need a cushion which is high enough. If you are really supple, you will then be able to lift both feet onto your inner thighs (lotus position). If you are less supple, you might manage one foot 'up' (half lotus). Many people need to have both feet on the floor, at least at first. When you get into this stance, you will feel how stable it is, and that it encourages a straight back; it is the position of alertness. But if you are not used to it, this way of sitting can be hard to maintain at first.

Whichever position you adopt — and only one of these three is recommended — you should sit about one metre from the wall, facing it with your eyes open and looking slightly downwards, with your hands either one in the other in front of you, or separated on the knees.

As you get into position, shrug your shoulders, loosen the muscles in your neck by rotating your head, and loosen the jaw, so that you don't begin the meditation tensed up. In the beginning, it may help your concentration if you control your breathing, making it slow and regular, with pauses before each breath in and out, but this is optional and may be discarded with practice. The room should have subdued light — not as bright as full daylight — but it should not be dark.

The group leader for this meditation has the role of time-keeper, so he or she will need a watch to signal the start and end of the meditation. He or she is also responsible for checking the position of each participant before the start of the meditation, making sure that backs are straight and knees are on the floor, if the sitting position is used. During the meditation, be alert for drooping backs; it is a sure sign that someone is being conquered by the 'enemies'. Quietly go round and straighten them without words and without disturbing other people. Twice in my experience, I have known people sitting on chairs to go to sleep and fall off them. If someone on a chair starts swaying, get there, quietly but quickly! (It is an advantage to sit on the floor rather than on a chair: you cannot fall anywhere!)

After the meditation, the group members should not rush into speech, but slowly stretch their legs and put the room back in order. Then, for the first meditation, and perhaps a few others, you can share 'experiences'. After a while, it is good to go straight into another exercise as soon as the group has re-assembled, without talking.

As they start to do this kind of meditation, people often say that they have just spent an uncomfortable half hour battling thoughts, and that it all seemed pointless. But an experience of this kind actually 'lift' the energy of the group.

It is a good idea to do the exercise in the daytime, somewhere where there is immediate access to a garden or nature spot. Then the group leader can send the group out after the meditation — still no talking — to look at the flowers, trees or view. As a result of the sitting, you will see that your perception has become enhanced; this is a pleasant and practical demonstration of its transformative effect.

After Zen meditation has been learned, it would be most valuable if the group incorporated it into its regular meetings, both for its own sake and, at the beginning of a session, in order to enhance the effect of other exercises. It is also a wonderful technique for individuals to adopt morning and/or evening, to prepare for or to release the day. As Sai Baba says: *"You are not the body, but the indestructible, eternal Atma (Essence) — Divinity itself."*

Exercise 7

Developing Intuition

This exercise is an easy way to support the growth of your 'inner view', and each other at the same time. It depends on bypassing rationality and letting your inner wisdom speak.

At first, this is strange for most people, for they think of rationality as the only means of control they have. Beyond rationality is ... what? All kinds of fears and anxieties come up. But, if you seek beyond rationality in the right direction, loving wisdom is to be found. How do you find the right direction? By preparing yourself for it in meditation. All this does not need to be ponderous, much less pretentious. The exercise can be treated very lightly.

You are going to describe your partner by using a house as the symbol. Talk about the house, without trying to interpret what comes to you at this stage. Your partner is going to write down everything you say about the house. But you are not going to go through a rational process, such as: this is what I think my partner is like; therefore this house would be most appropriate.

Instead, the exercise proceeds as follows: the group sits in pairs in a circle, with each pair facing each other. One partner, A, faces out, the other, B, faces into the circle. Each pair should be as far from the next as the room allows. (This exercise can be done outdoors, if there is a secluded, positive space, and it is a warm, quiet day. To discover 'positive' spaces, consult the Appendix, *Exercises in Nature.*) Each person should have pen and paper available.

Here are some words for the group leader:

Close your eyes and sit comfortably . . .
Take a few deep, relaxing breaths . . .
Begin to visualise or sense a light, filling this room, filling each of us and the whole space . . .
We ask that all we do be from this light, from the highest and for the highest good . . .
We ask that this exercise be blessed for the whole time it is taking place and give thanks that it is so . . .
Now, make an inner connection with your partner, a connection of non-judgment and unconditional love, aware of all, yet judging nothing . . .
Each of you is of the light and in the light . . .
*Now, B, open your eyes and take up your pen and pencil. A, **keep your eyes closed** and imagine B as if they were a house. As soon as a sense or image of a house comes into your mind, start describing it . . .*
For instance, how does it look from the outside? What state is it in? How does it stand in relation to other houses? Does it have a garden? If so, what sort? How do you get into this house? Then describe it inside. Go into more and more detail. Are there any rooms which are difficult to get into? Any cellars or attics? How is it furnished? Say everything you can, but don't wait till you have a full picture. Just start talking and allow your imagination to lead you. Don't bother with what it all means.
You have 15 minutes. Start as soon as you get an image.

The group leader keeps time. Some people find it easy and start talking at once; they often stimulate others. If someone is really having a hard time, you can go over to them and say (quietly), 'Any old house will do. Don't worry whether it's the right one', or something to reduce anxiety. Most people who hesitate are afraid of saying the wrong thing. If someone dries up and opens their eyes, encourage them to stay with eyes closed;

'Something more might come', or, 'See if you can get more detail about the house.'

After about twelve minutes, you can say:

If B has any questions about the house, you can ask them now. A, keep your eyes closed.

After about fifteen minutes, you say:

Time's up. Finish what you're saying and both of you close your eyes . . .
A, did you say everything that came to you, or did you hold back at all? If so, notice why . . .
B, did you write down everything that was said, or did you leave something out? . . .
If so, try to remember it and write it down later . . .
Now, inwardly thank your partner and release them. Open your eyes, but don't talk, please.

Now the group leader organises the Bs so that they move one place clockwise round the circle and are facing a new 'A' (This is to make it more difficult for B to think about what to say to A.)

A takes up pen and paper, and once more the partners close their eyes and the words of introduction are repeated. Don't skim over them, although you can reduce the number of 'specimen questions' if people have got the hang of it. The exercise then goes on as before. At the end, after 'inwardly thank your partner and release them', say:

We give thanks for the information we have received, the gifts that have been given.

Then everyone opens their eyes and the group leader instructs the Bs to move one more time round the circle. With their new partner, both A and B can share and discuss the 'house' they have received and if it means anything to them. The descriptions often contain surprising insights.

Notes

Most people find a house an easy symbol to work with. If the group enjoys the exercise, you can do it on another occasion, asking the 'readers' to imagine their partners with a circle of colours round them — their 'inner aura'. You can check if the colours are faint or thick, clear or cloudy, and so on. Perhaps the readers can attempt to interpret the meaning of the colours they see, again without 'thinking' about them.

If you do go on in this way, make sure that the group leader prepares the exercise beforehand and *never* leave out the introductory meditations and the giving of thanks afterwards. They are crucial, for they set the tone of what is being done.

Do not get hung up about what you will receive during such exercises. They may give you insights about yourself, but they are mainly to practise opening to intuition in a loving atmosphere. If you find yourself strongly resistant to something someone has said, there's a good chance it is important to you.

This is the kind of exercise that can lead to clairvoyant reading. Everyone is clairvoyant; but to give a good, clear, relatively accurate reading takes a lot of practice, so don't think you're a 'reader' after you've done it a couple of times.

The main purpose of this exercise is to open lovingly to intuition. Eventually, you'll feel able to trust it — the divine nature which guides your life. But don't rush! Allow yourself learning time with your friends, as you do these exercises together.

Exercise 8

Intuitive Verbal Healing

The next four exercises are a little more intense. By now, the group members should know each other better and have developed some love and trust together. They should also know that they can 'take risks in love', and, hopefully, that the group is a safe place for tears to flow if they want to. Everyone will have had a little practice in leading the group.

This exercise involves three aspects of our identities, so it is done in groups of three, with each person in turn playing the roles which represent these aspects:

• Our 'problem' part

This aspect is the part of us which does not yet feel like pure love, and so lives in 'getting and forgetting', causing us unhappiness and mood swings. This is the part that needs to be 'healed'. Notice that it is also a part that can surrender to healing, if ego allows it. Through the *surrender*, we can find grace and love. This aspect is here named 'Healee'.

• Our compassionate self

This aspect practises love by 'giving and forgiving' and is the 'Healer' in us.

• The Divine Self

This aspect is truth, waiting in bliss for us to join it; giving us the grace to be seemingly independent. This is the 'Observer', whose being enables the other two aspects to work, but is detached from problems and solutions, though not indifferent to them.

The group divides into triads, with the group leader keeping separate. 'Odd bodies' can be extra Observers in a group and get a healing afterwards, or, if there are two of them, can give and receive healing — at least doing two thirds of the exercise.

The procedure is as follows: each triad finds a space in the room and erects a symbolic 'barrier' to other groups, using chairs, blankets, or whatever comes to hand. Then they build a 'nest' with chairs or cushions, where they can be comfortable. There are going to be three 'healings' in the group and it can be quite intense, so have blankets to cuddle into and paper hankies to cry into, in case they are needed. It helps if everyone has read the instructions first.

The group leader begins the exercise by a short meditation to lift the energy level:

We close our eyes and make ourselves comfortable . . .
Take a few deep, slow breaths to calm and relax yourselves . . .
Now, let's see this room filled with light, light for each individual, each group and for the room as a whole . . .
We ask blessing for this exercise . . .
May everything we do come from the highest and be for the highest good . . .
May we be in the light for the whole duration of the exercise, so that each person receives that which they most need today . . .
We give thanks that it is so . . .
Visualise the other two members of your group. Connect with them from your heart, without judgment and with unconditional love . . .
Now open your eyes.

Each person in the group now thinks of a problem or challenge which they would like help with. It can be physical, psychological, emotional or spiritual. Don't share it yet!

The member of each triad become 'A','B' and 'C'.

When the group leader has arranged all this, he or she continues:

> *In this first part, A will share their problem, B will be the healer and C, the observer.*
>
> *When A has shared their problem, B will go round behind A, put their hands on A's shoulders, close their eyes and **wait**, without consciously thinking of any solutions. C will be with you, giving you both unconditional love and **total** attention, but **not getting involved**.*
>
> *OK, A, share your problem.*

When all the As have shared their problem and all the Bs are behind the As, that is, all triads are ready and waiting, the group leader says:

> *Now, B, allow healing words for A to come to you. Don't try to think if they are appropriate or not. Say anything that occurs to you. If you feel a story coming, tell it. If you see a picture, describe it. If you have a feeling, share it. If there's nothing, say that, too. Allow whatever comes to you to be the perfect thing for A.*
>
> *A, open yourself as much as you can to be healed.*
>
> *And C, support the process by giving A and B all your love and individual attention, but don't get involved.*
>
> *You've got about eight minutes. Off you go!*

During the eight minutes, the group leader makes sure anyone who needs it has paper hankies, and keeps in awareness what is happening in each triad. It is good to walk quietly near the different groups in turn, listen to a few words and then move on. If any healer opens their eyes and thinks they have finished, say quietly 'Stay there, something else might come.'

At six minutes, say, so all can hear:

Two minutes to go.

And at 8 minutes:

Finish off now . . .
B, return to your place, and everyone shut your eyes . . .
If you were A, could you accept the love given you in B's
words, or did you want something different? . . .
If you were B, could you allow yourself to say whatever
came to you, or did you censor yourself? . . .
If you were C, could you give your total attention to the
others? . . .
Just notice everything that happened; don't judge yourself
for it . . .
Now, open your eyes again, without talking . . .
This time, B will share their problem, after which C will go
behind B and put their hands on B's shoulders, close their
eyes and **wait***. A will give unconditional love and undi-*
vided attention.

Then lead the process exactly as before, making sure
not to mix up the letters, until:

Now open your eyes again, without talking . . .
Next, C will share their problem, after which A will go
behind C, put their hands on C's shoulders, close their eyes
and **wait***. B will give unconditional love and undivided*
attention.

The process is again repeated, until:

We give thanks for this time with our partners, for the grace
we have received, and for the insights we have been given.
We affirm our individual separateness.
Now open your eyes . . .
Thank your partners for their love and attention and share
with them how it felt for you.

Finally, bring the group back together and have at least one person from each group share what happened. End with a moment of silence to give thanks.

Notes

This exercise can be a moving experience, as well as giving quite strong insights into different aspects of being. It is important to try to be honestly aware of tendencies you may have, such as to compete to be a 'better' healer, or to resist — 'these words aren't right for me'. Remember, if you knew the solution to your problem, you wouldn't have it!

As Observer, did you wander, or get involved in what happened, or find yourself listening to someone else in another group, rather than giving full attention to your own partners? Try not to judge yourself for anything which you may have experienced. At the beginning, you set up the energy for the highest good. Trust that everything you received, gave or noticed was valuable in some way and accept yourself. This is also a practice of love.

In this exercise, through the role of healer, we are learning to open to our higher wisdom, by just saying whatever comes to mind (having first prepared ourselves with the opening meditations). Do the meditations with awareness and attention, open yourself in faith and the 'right' words will come; they really will. Learning to trust that it is so allows you to become guided and to live in grace.

For the Group Leader

This is quite a demanding exercise to lead. Try reading it through a few times, till you've really got the hang of it. Take it slowly and trust that you too are in the light and need not be nervous. It helps to have a little table with you, like the example below; otherwise, it is easy to get the letters mixed up and confuse everybody, which tends to dissipate the energy that the triads built up.

	Healee	Healer	Observer
1	A	B	C
2	B	C	A
3	C	A	B

Exercise 9

Spiritual Healing

You are not your body; but through your body may flow an inexhaustible stream of Divine energy. You are not your mind; but your mind may be filled with Divine knowing. You are not your feelings; but your heart may be filled with Divine Love.

Essentially, these are the experiences you are seeking when you practise spiritual healing. Since they are your highest attainments as a human being, the practice of healing is a conscious way of seeking, part of the spiritual path. Since most people's physique and mentality are not prepared for such energies to flow, the practice of healing is a way of developing them.

So the benefit of spiritual healing is not merely to the person healed, but also to the healer. Many books have been written about spiritual healing. *Healing in a group* is an exercise in compassion, a realisation that you are much more than you allowed yourself to be.

Everyone is capable of healing. No one who loves does not heal the loved one, unless the loved one is Divinity itself, perfection, whose Grace allows humanity to experience love, its essence.

This form of group spiritual healing is simple and safe. After you have learned the technique and practised it on each other, you can give your friends and acquaintances the benefit of a healing. You will find that healing is never tiring nor boring and that, in a subtle way, its practice changes you in your everyday life. It combines with compassion the qualities of concentration and intuition already developed in the previous exercises. Healing can be easily learned.

The group will need a small mattress and plenty of blankets and cushions; two mattresses if the group is larger than about seven or eight, when two healings can go on at the same time. The room should be warm and softly lit.

The group agrees on a leader for the healing. He or she is responsible for leading the group during the process of healing. But there is a preliminary training exercise for all to do, so that everyone is capable of taking the position of group leader in a healing, as their turn comes.

The training exercise is as follows: the group splits into triads as far as possible, with groups of four if there are 'extra' people. In these small groups you will practise:

1. preparing for a healing;
2. starting the healing off;
3. finishing the healing.

What is missed out in this practice is the healing itself. It is good to take notes, so that if you forget the procedure, when you are leading your first healing, you can briefly refer to them. In the practice, one person plays healer, one lies down, as if being healed and one plays assistant.

1. Preparation

Before any 'healing' takes place, the group sits in a circle round a candle to prepare itself through a guided meditation. Here is a form of words to use for the person playing healer:

> Let's close our eyes, sit upright and relax . . .
> We breathe deeply and slowly to centre ourselves . . .
> We sense a light filling us and the room, the light of Divine love . . .
> We ask that all our work this evening comes from this light . . .

We ask that we become channels for love to flow through us in appropriate measure and form, for us and for the person being healed . . .
We dedicate them our full attention and concentration so this love can flow . . .
We ask that everything comes from the highest, . . .
is for the highest good . . .
and is blessed for the entire time we are working . . .
We give thanks that it will be so. Now we will open our eyes and prepare for the healing.

2. Starting off

One of the group lies down, pretending to be a 'healee'. The lead healer gets into position; usually near the head of the healee is best, but this is not essential (it is a good position for contact with the rest of the group). He or she places the other 'healers' appropriately and leads the following meditation:

(Part A)
Let's close our eyes and centre ourselves in the light . . .
We make a connection of unconditional love and non-judgment amongst us, including X (the healee) . . .
For the duration of the healing, we will give X our total and undivided attention . . .

(Part B)
We ask that all unwanted energies from this healing may pass from us into the earth to be absorbed during the whole time the healing takes place. . .

(Part C)
We ask that we become pure channels of divine love for the healing, so that just the energy that X needs can flow through us, according to our capacity to pass it on . . .

Sometimes it feels more 'real' if parts B and C are

done with imagery, for example:

(Alternative B)
Let's imagine that we are trees, with roots going down deep into the earth . . .
These roots will take away any unwanted energy during the healing . . .

(Alternative C)
Let's imagine a column of light passing through us . . .
From the column, just the right amount is drawn off for this healing, passing down our arms, through our hands and/or into our voice, as necessary . . .

Since this is a 'practice', to learn the technique, the healing itself is by-passed and the triad goes on to Part 3.

3. Finishing

The lead healer says:

Now the healing is gently coming to a close . . .
Remove your hands from X, so gently that they don't even feel them going . . .
Release your connection with X, leaving all the energy of the healing with them . . .
directing any surplus energy into the earth . . .
and retaining all your own, personal energy . . .
Now, affirm your own regular identity by repeating your own name silently to yourself . . .
When you are ready, open your eyes.

The triad then checks if the lead healer has mentioned all the points in the above meditations and swaps around, until each person has practised the technique.

The reasons for formalising the technique come from experience. Parts 1 and 2(A) establish the group in light and love at the highest level on which it is capable of functioning, abolishing day to day criticisms and judgment of others.

Part 2(B) is necessary because healing does not only involve giving energy. The person being healed may release energy and you don't want to take that energy in. There is no point in the healee getting better and the healer getting worse!

Part 2(C) is to ensure that you don't, in your desire to heal, give your own physical energy to the person being healed, as this only results in the healee feeling temporarily stronger and you weaker! By being channels for Divine love you are involved with a limitless energy source benefiting both healers and healee.

Part 3 is important because, in the intensity of a healing, you sometimes bind yourselves together energetically. If you don't fully return to your own individual and distinct self, there can be a disorienting sensation of not knowing who you are!

Thus, these short meditations have a purpose and value for everyone in the group. If more than one healing is to be performed in an evening, Part 1 need only be done once, but, until the group is experienced, it is better to do it before every healing.

Having learned the preparatory meditations, we can now move to the real healing itself.

Doing a Healing

After Part 1 is completed, the lead healer welcomes the person to be healed and invites them to lie down on their back on the mattress. A healing can be performed in any position, but lying down full length on the back makes a 'healee' feel more open and vulnerable. It also allows the group to be around the person comfortably. Someone offers the healee a blanket and, if it is wanted, spreads it over them.

The lead healer then asks the healee to describe their problem. Everyone listens carefully and may ask for clarification, such as, 'How long has it been going on?'; 'What treatment have you already sought?'; 'Were there significant circumstances when it began?'; etc. This helps to relax the healee and indicates real interest.

Notice that we are all good at fabricating explanations of our problems which don't necessarily go to their source. In the healing, trust your intuition. Incidentally, the problem need not only be a physical complaint; one can have a healing for any problem, from the seemingly trivial to the seemingly devastating. Each problem is given equivalent attention by the healers. Who knows what is *really* hidden behind a superficial explanation?

Then the lead healer tells the healee:

All you need to do is to relax and be comfortable. Is it alright if we lay our hands on you during the healing?

Most people like this; it gives reassurance, but it is not essential. In a very few cases, people prefer no physical contact. The group leader continues:

I may share images with you during the healing, and we may make sounds or sing.

Then the lead healer leads the group into Part 2, to prepare for the healing.

In a group healing, the lead healer is a little like the conductor of an orchestra. The group obeys them implicitly. Even if, as an individual, you are not happy with what is going on, abide with it and share your feelings *afterwards*. Otherwise, the energy will be disrupted.

In the conductor's repertoire are:
• *energy passing through the hands* (which might have a colour or hue);
• *sharing of images*;
• *verbal guided meditation or symbols or 'stories'* (only told by the leader);
• *sounds* made by the leader, which the group takes up

for as long as the lead healer thinks appropriate, or even *songs*, which the group also takes up.

As lead healer, you 'hold the energy' in the room, your faith ensuring that it expresses Divine love and light alone.

The basic theme is *harmony* of divine love flowing through the healing group to the healee, with whatever energy the healee releases flowing back into the earth. Everyone has their own way of leading a healing; everyone has a different nuance to give. 'Strangely enough', usually the healer and healee are 'just right' for each other.

After completing Part 2, the lead healer opens their eyes gently and tells the group to do so as well. From then on, you must trust your intuition implicitly. You position the group members around the healee as it feels right to you, and instruct them to place their hands on the healee's body accordingly. (There shouldn't be heavy hand pressure or any kind of massage. You are working with energy.) Eyes can then be closed again.

Next, you begin to allow the energy to flow through the group to the healee. If it seems to have a colour, *tell the group to channel that colour!* After a while, you may 'feel' words, or 'see' images; *share them!* You may, at some point, sense a sound waiting to be made. *Instruct the group to make it with you!* When it seems sufficient, *stop!* Sometimes there is humour. Sometimes there is total silence. *Trust your intuition!* You have set its source with your preparatory meditation.

Eventually, when it seems that the healee has absorbed all the energy they are able to take, bring the healing to a close, with Part 3.

After some moments, ask the healee to say how they feel. Don't let them go into details or ask for explanations. The very best thing for them is to go straight to bed. If this is possible, one of the group — a friend if one is there — can be asked to take them. If the healee is part of the group and the group is going to do another healing, lie them down in a corner somewhere to relax and doze. Don't let them take part in the next healing.

All this is done because it is easy to 'talk away' the energy of a healing, or lose it in further activity. A group channelling love is powerful treatment; it needs to be absorbed. After the healee is out of earshot, the group can discuss the impressions and images they had. If the person who received the healing belongs to the group, they can share at the next meeting.

Notes about Healing

This way of performing healings is simple and uncomplicated. It can be adapted easily to do individual healings. (You can do the preparatory meditations silently, telling the healee that you are preparing yourself. But never skim over them!) You will never be given more than you can handle. Trust this and have confidence.

Sometimes a healing releases stored pain and grief. If a person starts crying heavily during the work, encourage them to breathe deeply, until they return to their normal breathing. Very occasionally, a healee may have tremors as the energy 'works'. Again, lovingly regulate the breathing and the tremors will subside after a while. Have confidence in your preparatory meditations. You are a pure channel of Divine love; nothing can go wrong. You don't need any intermediate 'beings' or 'helpers' for the healing. Divine love itself is flowing through you. It is your highest, limitless energy — your ultimate truth.

Here are some pitfalls to avoid. Do not get hung up about results. Healing works only to the degree that all parties allow it. Trying hard doesn't make for better healing; it just tires you out. Relax, allow the energy to flow through you. That way it will work best.

Perhaps the healee is just starting to work on their problem. Your healing will be a contribution, though much still remains to be done. Perhaps the healee is just ready to release a problem; then the results may be more dramatic, but your contribution was only the very last touch to the break through. A stone doesn't necessarily shatter the first time you hit it. But the tenth blow which breaks it may only be a tap; the other nine have done the main work.

Secondly, anything that happens is love's work, not your ego's. Don't bathe yourself in the healee's praise: 'I feel wonderful, the pain's all gone', or feel useless if they say: 'It's just as bad as before'. Your responsibility is to channel unconditional love as appropriately as you can and to lead the group through in harmony. That is all.

If you like to practise healing, be careful not to confuse it with self-confidence. A person who only feels good when they are healing generates around them illnesses to heal. Such a healer's good feelings depend upon other people's pain; don't be a 'do-gooder', but do channel love! That will do you good and bring you closer to your ultimate truth, Love itself.

'Miracle' healings are a product of faith, confidence and grace; perfect confidence on the part of the healer, perfect faith on part of the healee. As Jesus said: "Your faith has made you whole." Such healings are a result of perfection, so let yourself be a trainee and enjoy the wonderful atmosphere, good experiences and fine company of doing healings with a group. You are on your way.

Exercise 10

Intuition Clinic

In two of the exercises so far, you have supported your partner verbally by describing their 'house' and by giving them a verbal healing (in the triad exercise). This verbal work can be developed into something you do in a group with others, an intense and uplifting experience.

The group divides into subgroups of 4 or 5 people (3 are too few, and 6 would made the subgroup too big), but you don't need an overall group leader for this exercise, except to start the proceedings off. Once the groups are established, you can come together for a preparatory meditation, which *does* need a guide. As usual, this is to set the energy for the work and everyone should be familiar with it by now. The group sits in a circle round the candle:

> *Relax, close your eyes . . .*
> *Breathe slowly and consciously to bring yourself fully present . . .*
> *See an inner light shining from the group, filling the whole room with light . . .*
> *We ask that everything we do in this exercise is in the light, comes from the highest and is for the highest good . . .*
> *We ask that the exercise be blessed, so that each member receives exactly the information they require, in ways they can accept . . .*
> *We give thanks that these things will be so . . .*
> *Now, gently, open your eyes.*

The subgroups then form, each having the maximum available space (but stay in the room you have filled with light). Everyone will need paper and pen and there should be enough chairs and/or cushions and blankets to make yourselves comfortable.

One person in the subgroup now becomes temporary group leader and another, X, becomes the one to share a 'problem', again, of any sort. The subgroup reforms in a fan shape, *so that everyone is directly facing X*, close together, giving each member the same access to X.

After the problem is shared, the first leader guides the group in a little meditation, as follows:

We close our eyes and feel the light embracing the group . . .
We make a connection together, of non-judgment and
unconditional love . . . and allow our highest intuition to
give us information relevant to the problem that X has just
shared . . . We give thanks for this opportunity . . .
Whoever is ready can begin.

The subgroup stays with eyes closed, except for X, who takes up pen and paper. The temporary group leader can both take part and keep aware of what is going on. Bypassing the rational thought process and trusting the preparatory meditations, each person now shares the images or words that come to them, one person at a time.

If you feel brave, inwardly ask for an interpretation of symbols or images, but don't let your reason take over; the aim is to work with Divine intelligence. Also, don't think anything that comes is silly or inappropriate; just share it. When all the 'readers' have shared, have another go. You may well find that something someone else has said stimulated you. Don't forget to keep your eyes closed the whole time.

X writes everything down. When it all seems complete, and without leaving a ponderous pause, the temporary group leader says:

Is everyone finished? . . .
We give thanks for the information we received . . .
and release the special connection with X, sensing our own
name ringing within us . . .
We now open our eyes.

Without any chatter, the group rearranges itself so that another member becomes X and someone else is temporary leader. Then the whole procedure is repeated, including the meditations at the beginning and the end. Since this exercise involves concentration and a lot of sitting still, it is good to take a little break after the second session, without losing the atmosphere or talking about the work.

In turn, the remaining members of the group take on the roles of X and temporary group leader, repeating the meditations for each session, till all have had their turn at being 'read' and leading the group.

The final temporary group leader then adds the following sentence to the concluding meditation:

We give thanks for each other's loving attention and
caring . . .
And we open our eyes.

After such a period of intensive concentration, the group usually feels tired but uplifted, ready for a group hug and home!

Study what you received when you were X. If it feels irrelevant or cryptic, read it last thing at night and ask for a dream about it. You may get insights that way. Don't get hung up if somebody says something you feel is totally wrong. Just write it down and notice it. Remember, as in all the other exercises, the point is to learn to open yourself to Spirit in different ways. Each of you is learning: the subgroup members to contact higher wisdom; the Xs, acceptance and surrender. Learn to accept that the temperament of each member of the group will 'colour' their words or actions. Let them be who they are—they'll change faster that way — and expect the same for yourself.

After repeating this exercise several times in the group, you may feel confident enough to ask some friends in to 'have a clinic'. Do explain to them carefully what is going on, and don't let them take part in the group apart from receiving information. They need more experience first. Believe it or not, by the time you've come to the point of asking friends in for Exercises 9 and 10, you will have moved a lot in yourself. You'll find you have new insights, new challenges, and more powerful tools for looking at the world and a greater degree of detachment from it. The light in your eyes will be glowing brighter!

Exercise 11

Intuitive Writing

This exercise is the basis of learning how to channel — to receive messages from a higher source. It is not necessary for any channelling to actually occur, but the exercise is a further way of learning how to trust. We cannot demand to receive messages from a higher source, for we are still ego-bound and not in control of that source. We can 'set' our energy to the highest and see what happens. This is what is done in the exercise.

It starts with a meditation to set the energy at the highest, and then, for a set period of time, the group members allow whatever comes to each individual to be written down. This is not the same as 'automatic' writing, where the hand writes without the volition of the writer. That sometimes happens in this exercise, but mostly, words, images or ideas come, letting the source, our highest consciousness, play on the mind to give us what we need.

What we need is not always what we want. In one group a member had always been a 'good' girl, and was most upset when she found, during her first attempt, that she just wanted to scribble and slash the pen across the paper. Of course, this was what she needed to break free from the straitjacket of worldly 'goodness' she'd imposed on herself throughout her life. Later, she received some beautiful messages.

The challenge is to abandon judgment and censorship of what goes on, and dare to write down whatever may come. Maybe, for you, the 'right' thing just now is to free material from your unconscious mind. Or to break away from the conformity of your education and be creative. Or to exercise your imagination in the realms of fantasy. Some people write 'stream of consciousness' passages. Others draw. Some write frenetically for the whole duration, others jot down a few 'key' words. Occasionally, people find themselves writing in strange 'scripts'.

The important thing is not to say that only such and such is appropriate and enter into self-censorship or judgment. In some cases it may be appropriate to write nothing at all, but usually this indicates that the ego has entered into a game of resistance and censorship. If that appears to be happening, write it down, too: 'I'm getting nothing'; 'I'm resisting putting my thoughts down', as this often acts as a bridge to writing. Trust the meditation. You may be being shown how your thought-forms stifle your potential.

Here is how to do the exercise.

Part 1: Writing

Everyone will need a pen and plenty of paper, with a spare pile in the room, in case someone runs out. A writing board or large book may help. If there are tables available, chairs can be set round them. Then everyone seeks out a 'good' position for themselves, settles down with pen and paper and the group leader begins, as follows:

Close your eyes, relax your bodies, allow your deep, slow breathing to centre you . . .
Let's imagine a light, shining from each one of us and filling the room, the light of Divine love, our highest Self . . .
We ask that this light be our source in this exercise, and that we receive exactly what is appropriate for us to receive today . . .
We ask that the exercise be blessed; that, for its whole duration we are guided by the light and are in the light . . .
In this knowledge, we joyfully open ourselves to whatever

comes to us, without restraint or self-censorship . . .
We give thanks for this opportunity . . .
Now, open your eyes and begin writing as soon as
anything comes to you, thought, image, symbol, story,
good advice, whatever. Don't wait for things to be
complete in your head before you start writing. Just
begin. You have 25 minutes.

(Twenty-five minutes is an appropriate amount of time for a group to work with.)

The group leader should participate, but with half an eye of awareness on the rest of the group, in case their support is needed by someone with strong emotions. Intervene only if the process is really disrupting the energy in the room.

At the end, the group leader says:

The time is over . . .
Finish the sentence you are writing . . .
Everyone close their eyes and do an inner check. Did you
write everything that came to you, or did you think some
things were inappropriate and leave them out? If so, notice
it without judging yourself . . .
We give thanks for this time and for everything we have
received . . .
Releasing this state by repeating our name to ourselves
inwardly, we open our eyes.

Part 2: Sharing

The second part of the exercise is to share what has been received. It is just as powerful as the first part. There is no obligation on a person to read out or show what has come to them, but if the group is *loving, supportive and non-judgmental*, all will find themselves able to share.

The group members form a circle round the candle, get comfortable (for the sharing may last a long time), then the group leader starts with an attunement, all holding hands:

> *We see the room filled with light and give thanks for this time of sharing together . . .*
> *As we share, let's remember that no one has received anything 'better' than anyone else, that each person got what was right for them and that sharing gives us the collective wisdom the group received . . .*
> *Let's now open our eyes.*

Before they share what they have received, each person explains what happened for them during the exercise. After they have finished, questions or comments are in order, but no criticism or judgmental statements. Anything like that breaks trust and can kill the atmosphere very quickly. Be supportive to every person in the group, whether they 'heard God's words', or got nothing at all. Every group member gives each sharer their full attention.

At the end, a normal closing attunement finishes the session.

Notes

The exercise can be repeated by the group every so often. You will discover that what you receive changes and develops with time. Also, intuitive writing can be done individually at home.

If you try it, remember *never to skim over on the meditation*, for that sets your energy to the highest level. Always allow a limited time period, after which you stop, no matter how eager you are to continue. The physical body gets tired, holding such a high energy. There is always another time and the Higher Self won't go away or forget! As you practise, you can extend the time you take. Remember also that you don't need to rush to write down everything that comes. Find your own calm and relaxed pace. Nothing will be lost; but by rushing, you might have difficulty deciphering what you wrote!

For some people, the love that these messages express is very moving. Perhaps you haven't realised that *you* are loved in this very personal way, that God *is* with you. Eventually, you may develop confidence in this higher contact. The way to do so is by checking it carefully against your day-to-day experience. If it consistently does not contradict your common sense and conscience, it can become a way to assist in guiding your life.

It has become fashionable and popular to 'channel' wisdom from 'disembodied beings'. This may happen to you; but surely, it would be more preferable to channel from the highest source of all, the reality of life which is your own essence — Divine love itself. It will joyfully express itself through you if you give it the opportunity. That is the point of all these exercises.

There is something of glamourous consumerism about the 'New Age' tendency to 'get wisdom from the masters', play with crystals and various 'magical' phenomena. This book is written for those who want to go beyond all that and find Truth and the reality of Divine love in themselves. Seek the highest and you will find it.

Continuing with the Group

The foregoing exercises provide a basis for an ongoing spiritual group, centred itself on spiritual healing and intuitive counselling, as described in Exercises 9 and 10. The group may meet regularly, fortnightly or monthly. But always begin with a meditation and spiritual sharing — make sure you avoid gossip and general sharing about the state of the world, etc. Then it can continue with healings and/or intuitive clinic. If group members have other exercises of value they'd like to introduce, that is fine, although it is best to have an ongoing theme.

As soon as the group develops enough confidence, friends should be invited to visit for healings or counselling. It concentrates the mind wonderfully to have to work with someone from *outside*, and gives a sense of service to the activity. With more experience, you may also want to work with strangers, who have been recommended by those you have already practised with.

After a while — perhaps in a year or two — the 'natural life' of the group will come to an end. Each member will then put the experience which they have gained from it to work in their ongoing lives; some may even go on to be healers or spiritual counsellors. So let the group go, with gratitude, and without regret.

Afterword

Working with these exercises, repeating them, and expanding from them, will provide a means of focussing the activities of the 'good company' you need, and help to strengthen your spiritual commitment. They can increase your confidence in the practice of love.

As you grow in strength, take what you learn in the group out into life. Life is the biggest exercise you have to take part in. No one can evade the challenge, but it helps to approach it consciously. Approach life seeking the ephemeral and it will mirror the ephemeral back to you. Come the day that your life ends, and you will have nothing. All will have been wasted, all will have to be repeated!

Approach life seeking happiness through love and it will unfold for you like a great story book, each page showing the way from 'here' to 'there'. Although, when you finally get 'there', you will find that you are still 'here'! However your consciousness will be totally transformed so that you see with God's eyes — your own true eyes.

Don't be faint-hearted. Above all, don't think of yourself as a miserable, hopeless sinner. There are bound to be many mistakes and setbacks as you explore life. But see them for what they are — mistakes and setbacks. Resolve to learn; forgive yourself. Aspire to love now. You don't need to postpone it for other lifetimes. *It is offered to you now.* Set out on the voyage of life's journey to love and you will reach the harbour. Happiness begins to be yours as soon as you set off, for you have a purpose which will constantly engage you, never bore you, and will inflame you with transformation.

The journey from self to Self is exciting. It doesn't

take place in a church, monastery or temple — they are but spaces where you can breathe calmly for a moment. The journey begins as soon as you wake up and goes on until your head touches the pillow and your eyes close — even then it goes on, as you absorb the teachings and opportunities the day has brought.

The message underlying each part of this book is: change your focus from the desires, objects, and connections of the outer world to the love that is the essence of all these things. Then, the outer things become your servants on your path to the realisation of love, not powerful masters which beset and tempt you on your way.

'Good company' strengthens your courage, helping you to be aware that a deeper truth lies behind outer forms. Devotion provides you with the easiest way to transcend your ego, so that it gradually becomes redundant.

Seek love; understand it; practise it . . . until one day you know it as your very nature. Then the happiness which you experienced in your search will become the bliss of discovery. You will be an empowered servant of humanity, knowing your path and freely choosing it!

Appendix

Exercises in Nature

Nature is a reflection of love, an aspect of the Divine system clothed in form. These forms can strike a chord of beauty in our hearts, uplifting us. For the so-called 'Earth peoples', especially the Native Americans and Australian Aboriginals, the natural world was a temple, infused with the Great Spirit, chalice of the Dream Time. For Western civilizations, on the other hand, nature has for a long time been something to be conquered and then ruthlessly exploited. The result is the contemporary ecological crisis.

In order to rectify this, the ecological movement is not enough. We need to learn once more to find reverence in nature, to be moved by love for her, and to expand our awareness of the Divinity expressed in natural forms. Only then will the devastation of nature become untenable and our environment recover.

So here are a few exercises, derived from the Native American tradition, that a group can do together. They are exercises which will help us to develop this reverence.

Finding a Power Spot

Choose a pleasant day for an outing together; take a picnic. It shouldn't be too hot, nor rainy, nor extremely windy, but a day which will allow all of you to give pleasurable attention to the country. Go to a place removed from urban noise and bustle, where there won't be many people around. It doesn't have to be a famous beauty spot but, if someone in the group has a 'special' place they like, and it meets the above requirements, that will be a good place.

Having arrived at the chosen spot and organized yourselves, the group leader for the day leads an attunement, with the group standing in a circle:

Let's close our eyes . . .
Breathe deeply and slowly and become calm . . .
Let's feel an inner light surrounding us, shining from the circle and the country around . . .
In this light, we now ask blessing for all our activities today . . .
May we be open, with respect and reverence for the experiences nature gives us . . .
We come to this spot in peace and goodwill and ask the spirits of nature here to work with us and be our guides, all the time we are here . . .
Let's listen a little to the sounds around us . . .
Let's feel the sun and wind on our faces . . .
Now, we open our eyes.

The next thing is for everybody to separate and start a slow ramble, allowing the feet to take you wherever they 'want' to go, and stopping to look at this and that.

When you come to a spot that draws you, sit down there for a few minutes. How does it feel? If, after five minutes or so, you feel just as you did before, then you have found a neutral spot. If you feel slightly restless and irritable, you have found a spot 'unfriendly for you'. If you have a definite, palpable sense of well-being, you have found a positive or 'power' spot for you. You'll be surprised how easy this is, if you don't let your rationality get in the way!

Carry on exploring till you have definitely identified places of all three types. Then return to one of your positive 'places of power' and sit there for some time, enjoying it, letting it drain tension and stress from you. Before you leave your spot, have a moment of inner attunement and give thanks to nature.

After about two hours, return to the group so everyone can share their experiences.

Learning to find beneficial spots in nature is a major step forward. You can 'make friends' with such a spot and, once you know how to find one, you will be able to go out alone and find calm and balance in such a place. Some spots are in general 'human friendly', and others human unfriendly'. Many are neutral. But some spots will be personally friendly, so you can feel a well-being there which other people may not.

Always, when you go out like this, spend time in an attunement to the light within you and invoke the aid of the nature spirits of the place. It will calm and sensitize you, and alert them to a friend. After a while, you will be able to feel the value for you of other places; where you work and live, for example. When people were closer to nature, they intuitively chose good locations for buildings and places of worship. Indeed, it became an art in China (*Feng Shui*).

But nowadays, almost all buildings are located for purely commercial reasons and some of them are in very 'unfriendly' spots. People wonder why they get ill, depressed and irritable. An unfriendly location can contribute to such distress.

Using Your Power Spot

Later the same day, or on another day, the members of the group may, after an attunement, return to one of their beloved spots, bringing paper and pen with them.

Having settled yourself down in your pleasant place, begin to examine it in very close detail, focussing on the detail and form of little plants, the movements of insects on the ground, the way the spot lies in relation to its horizon, trees, rocks and natural features. Notice how the sun strikes the vegetation and throws certain parts into relief. If you like, allow your imagination to build pictures and symbols from all these shapes and forms.

In doing this, you will be making a 'close connection' with the natural world, something even country ramblers usually fail to do. You are not doing it for some botanical or zoological purpose, but for the enjoyment of the intimacy itself. You may find yourself suddenly moved by the meanderings of a beetle; or you may 'make friends' with a tree or plant, which seems especially warm and connected to you.

After about an hour of sitting — most people cannot concentrate for any longer — take your pen and paper and start writing down whatever comes to you: it may be a description of the place; or perhaps your imagination weaves a story ; perhaps a poem comes. Perhaps you start imagining how this spot was hundreds, thousands, millions of years ago: write it down. Perhaps you 'hear' messages from the nature spirits around — the energies organizing the growth of plants and life of minerals. In the special space of your power spot, spend half an hour or an hour jotting down all your impressions.

The group can come together for lunch and share all these writings in the afternoon. Or do the writing one afternoon and share together 'at home' in the evening. Through such writing you become more aware, more connected, more loving to the natural world.

Using the Power Spot to Make Inner Contact with the Natural World

The world of water, rocks, earth, plants and animals has little consciousness in the sense that we know it. It is, and goes on being. In place of individual consciousness are the regulating *energies* of the natural forms. All peoples close to nature symbolize these as invisible inhabitants of nature spots; fairies, leprechauns, elves, gnomes, trolls, and so on. Some old people in remote areas still claim to be able to 'see' such beings, but they are mostly relegated to fairy stories and fantasy novels.

By being still in a positive power spot, we can develop a strong rapport with the energies governing nature; and through it, love and respect for the wonder of the natural world and the essential oneness underlying all this; Divine love.

As usual, the group starts with an attunement, then separates to seek positive power spots.

At your spot, settle down, feel the well-being from the 'good vibes', and begin to focus your attention on one point. Perhaps it is the branch of a tree, the shape of a plant, a spot framed by leaves, or an area of ground close by. Then you spend an hour just gazing lovingly at that spot, not straining the eyes, but moving as little as possible. You are not seeking anything except loving rapport, but, in time, what you are seeing may subtly change. At the least you will become entranced by the scene you see; perhaps you will 'see' lines of energy flowing around your point; perhaps a miniature 'alternative reality' will form itself for you. You may have visions; or receive advice.

After your time, close your eyes, make your breathing conscious, and give thanks. Then walk back to the group for a sharing.

Through this kind of practice you will gradually become not just a nature lover, nor just someone aware of ecological crises; but someone *living now in the oneness of all life*, with a respect for each of its forms. Not to leave litter around is no longer just part of the 'Country Code', for instance. It is simply unthinkable.

Nature as Healer and Therapist

Sun Bear taught people in emotional pain or trauma

to find a hole in the ground and howl into it, releasing the problem to Mother Earth. Similarly, this exercise enlists nature as a supporter, helping us to move on. As with the other exercises, it involves intuitive rapport.

The group attunes in an appropriate nature spot. For this exercise, even a large garden will do. Each member finds a partner and shares a problem or challenge they would like support to resolve. This is done in order to articulate the problem and fix it firmly in the forefront of consciousness.

When everyone is ready, the group comes together again and stands in a circle. The day's group leader begins the following short meditation:

> *Close your eyes . . .*
> *Become calm, by breathing slowly and deeply . . .*
> *In love and respect for the natural world, we ask the co-operation of the natural energies of this place for assistance in solving these challenges we face . . .*
> *We open ourselves for this assistance for the duration of the exercise . . .*
> *And give thanks for it . . .*
> *Now, we open our eyes and wander off, letting our feet carry us, stopping where it feels appropriate and being open for experiences, symbols, and insights given to us from the natural world around us.*

Everyone goes off on their 'healing walk'. After a pre-arranged time (half an hour to an hour), the members return, bringing with them anything that feels appropriate (and doesn't damage the locality by the taking) to share what happened to them during their wanderings. It is a good feeling to discover that natural forces will co-operate with humans if respected and loved, and that such co-operation may be mutually beneficial.

These exercises are not part of any 'shamanic path', but a way of practising love, respect, co-operation, and closeness with nature and enhancing a sense of oneness with all life. All these qualities are involved in spiritual development and bring benefit to all beings.

Further Reading

There are so many books and many different approaches to spirituality, even apart from the established religious traditions. It is important that study does not become a substitute for practice; but books can, of course, guide and stimulate. Here I have listed only a few of the books that have guided and stimulated me, in no sort of order or priority.

• The four gospels of the *New Testament*.

• *Original Blessing* by Matthew Fox (a Christian approach that is not 'sin centred').

• *The Gnostic Gospels* by Elaine Pagels (describes a rich and varied Christian tradition about which, until recently, we had very little information).

• *The Course in Miracles* (a channelled book, purportedly from Jesus Himself; it's all there, but rather heavy going).

• *Siddharta* by Herman Hesse (a brilliant fictional account of the search for enlightenment).

• *Journey to Ixtlan* by Carlos Castaneda (all his books are fascinating, but, for me, this one is the best; consciousness training from a master, using the nature tradition).

• *Selling Water by the River* by Jiyu Kennett (a manual of Zen training).

• *God Spoke to Me* and other books by Eileen Caddy (channelled wisdom, pure and beautiful).

• *The Holy Man and the Psychiatrist* by Samuel Sandweiss (a very impressive introduction to Sathya Sai Baba and His teaching).

• *Sathya Sai Speaks*, eleven volumes of discourses by Sai Baba, transcribed by N. Kasturi and translated from Telegu (here is the essence, spoken to all kinds of audi-

ences in India; the revised editions, just coming out, are
much easier to read).
• *Discourses on the Bhagavad Gita* by Sathya Sai Baba (34
discourses to students by Sai Baba, beautifully edited by
Al Drucker — the quintessence of Sai Baba's teaching).

Introducing Findhorn Press

Findhorn Press is the publishing business of the Findhorn Community which has grown around the Findhorn Foundation, co-founded in 1962 by Peter and Eileen Caddy and Dorothy Maclean. The first books originated from the early interest in Eileen's guidance over 20 years ago and Findhorn Press now publishes not only Eileen Caddy's books of guidance and inspirational material, but many other books, and it has also forged links with a number of like-minded authors and organisations.

For further information about the Findhorn Community and how to participate in its programmes please write to:
The Accommodation Secretary
Findhorn Foundation
Cluny Hill College, Forres IV36 0RD, Scotland
tel. +44 (0)1309-673655 fax +44 (0)1309 673113
e-mail reception@findhorn.org

For a complete catalogue, or for more information about Findhorn Press products,
please contact :

Findhorn Press
The Park, Findhorn, Forres IV36 0TZ , Scotland
tel. +44 (0)1309-690582 fax +44 (0)1309-690036
e-mail thierry@findhorn.org

Books about the Findhorn Community . . .

THE KINGDOM WITHIN (£8.95)   isbn 0 905249 99 2
A Guide to the Spiritual Work of the Findhorn Community
Compiled and edited by Alex Walker

This collection of writings about the history, work, beliefs
and practices of the Findhorn Foundation and its associated
community of spiritual seekers offers a vision of hope, inspiration and encouragement. With contributions by David
Spangler, William Bloom, Dorothy Maclean, Peter and Eileen
Caddy amongst others, this book covers topics which include
nature and ecology, the art of living in community, the relationship of 'new age' thought to formal religion, and co-operation with the spiritual worlds. The world is hungry for the
hope and inspiration this book brings — and so are you!

THE FINDHORN GARDEN (£9.95)   isbn 0 905249 63 1
Pioneering a New Vision of Humanity and Nature in Cooperation
by The Findhorn Community

The story of the early days of the Findhorn Community and
its communications with the nature kingdoms. Peter and
Eileen Caddy's experiences as co-founders of the community,
Dorothy Maclean's contact with the devas, R. Ogilvie Crom-
bie's (ROC's) meetings with Pan and the Elemental Kingdom,
and the wisdom of David Spangler and other combine to give
a unique perspective on the relationship between humans
and nature.

THE FINDHORN COMMUNITY (£8.95)   isbn 0 905249 77 1
by Carol Riddell

The author traces the community's development over the
years and gives a clear picture of the community today and
the new businesses and independent projects springing up
around it. The second half of the book includes a number of
intimate and revealing interviews with members, both young
and old, who share their lives and experiences of living in
this incredible community.

FOUNDATIONS OF A SPIRITUAL COMMUNITY (£5.95)
by Eileen Caddy isbn 0 905249 78 X

Guidance that helped a family living in a tiny caravan develop into an international spiritual community. The central principle of turning within to find the true source of faith, inspiration and love makes this book relevant not only for those building a spiritual community but also for all who live ordinary lives in our wider society.

THE SPIRIT OF FINDHORN (£5.95)
by Eileen Caddy isbn 0 905249 97 6

This book offers a brief history of how Eileen gave up everything to follow her inner voice as well as sharing much of the guidance and wisdom which supported Eileen through the early days of her spiritual transformation and the birth of the Findhorn Community.

Guidebooks for Growth Together . . .

Guidebooks for Growth Together is a new collection of books launched by Findhorn Press in the spring 1995. It consists of books addressed both to individuals and to groups who are looking for practical tools to help them on their spiritual path.

The Path to Love is the Practice of Love is one of the first two books of the collection. Published simultaneously:

JOURNEYS WITHIN (£6.95)   isbn 1 899171 35 5
Source-Book of Guided Meditations
by Lisa Davis
Aimed at both individuals and groups needing help with guided meditations, this book gives the reader support in how to begin, conduct and end meditations. It offers the opportunity to choose a topic from a variety of subjects which can be recorded and used as required. For anyone who is new to guided meditations or who has ever felt insecure or hesitant about leading them. It also gives opportunities for experienced meditators to expand their repertoire, with topics such asTarot, Colour, Chakras and Healing.

There are more books in preparation for the autumn of 1995...

New from Findhorn Press . . .

THE CHRIST SPARKS (£4.95)   isbn 1 899171 15 0
The Inner Dynamics of Group Consciousness
by William Bloom

As we move into the 21st century, humanity is experiencing
vast and difficult changes. The call for help has gone out to
the universe and the Christ Sparks - a swarm of conscious-
nesses from another system and dimension - have answered
this call. Over the last 25 years they have incarnated into individuals, groups, communities and nations and, using William
Bloom as a channel, they now provide startling new knowledge and vision. For anyone who has ever wondered why
couples are splitting up or how to affect the policies of
nations - consult the Christ Sparks!

*"William Bloom is one of the outstanding spiritual teachers of our
time. This book further reflects his deep range of inner knowledge
and the gift of his spirit."*   David Spangler

CLAP ONE HAND FOR THE BIG BANG (£5.95)
The Integration of Science and Spirit   isbn 1 899171 05 3
by Ian Pullen

This book is written as an invitation to join the author on a journey of exploration between the self and the universe. Thanks
to his sense of humour, it's a very enjoyable journey. Aimed at
the large section of society who are seeking purpose in their
lives, this books brings together traditionally conflicting view-
points of science and spirituality, helping us to see the logic in
in spirituality and the 'magic' in science.

"Original, easy to read and interesting...a winner"
                                        Right Reverend Alan Burns

Mail order information

In the UK, free postage & packing
In Europe, add £1 per book
Rest of the world, add £2 per book

Payment: by cheque made out to Findhorn Press, or
by Visa or Mastercard (please give number and expiry date)

Please send/phone/fax/e-mail your order to
Findhorn Press Mail Order
The Park, Findhorn, Forres IV36 0TZ , Scotland
tel. +44 (0)1309-690582 fax +44 (0)1309-690036
e-mail thierry@findhorn.org